How children learn 3
Contemporary thinking and theorists

by Linda Pound

Contents

Published by Practical Pre-School Books, A Division of MA Education
St Jude's Church, Dulwich Road, Herne Hill, London, SE24 0PB
Tel: 020 7738 5454

www.practicalpreschoolbooks.com

Illustrations: Cathy Hughes

© MA Education 2009

ISBN: 978-1-90457-588-7

Introduction

This book considers the contribution made by contemporary theorists and writers to current theories and understandings about how children learn and develop. It seeks to encourage reflection about the ideas each of us holds and the impact this has on the way we support learning and development.

As we saw in both *How Children Learn and How Children Learn 2*, theories can be rooted in research and experimentation or they can be philosophical and hypothetical. Whatever their basis, the importance of observation is a common strand in the work of many theorists who were interested in finding out how children learn. All the theories, ideas and movements explored in this book were developed by theorists and thinkers who observed how people, including children, learn.

The focus of the first of these books was generally on individual theorists - such as Jean Piaget or Susan Isaacs. In addition, there were some sections devoted to influential educational approaches such as High/Scope and Waldorf Steiner education. A further category involved sections which explored important aspects of early education such as learning through play or emotional intelligence.

The second book focused on trends and developments rather than individual theorists. It considered the way in which ancient theories have impacted on current thinking as well as exploring the influence of a wide range of progressive twentieth century ideas. This book mostly looked at the way in which theories about literacy, talking, intelligence and creativity have grown out of other people's theories, and then gone on to develop new thinking on a subject.

About this book

■ This book, the third in the series, focuses on thinkers and theorists who are currently influencing ideas about the learning and development of young children. These people will be listed alphabetically. In the second part of the book a range of related topics will be explored and these will also be listed alphabetically. These include a number of topics which are of particular interest to today's practitioners.

■ The sections will follow a common pattern - with some key facts to place the theory or theorist in a context. The theory is explained and the titles of some of their main publications listed. Theory will be linked to practice with examples where relevant and a comments box in each section is designed to encourage you to analyse critically what you have read.

■ There are a great many connections between different theories and these links will be highlighted - encouraging you to go beyond the page you are reading. I hope the book will make you want to delve deeper, becoming more reflective and finding out more about children's learning.

■ In writing about contemporary theorists I am conscious of the inevitable distortions and omissions which inevitable occur when attempting to synthesize large and complex bodies of work. I apologise in advance for any such errors and hope that they will be understood and forgiven. I also apologise to those that were left out.

Note to students:

Every effort has been made to ensure that you have all the information you will need to cite sources in your essays and projects. You will need to rearrange these references in your written work in order to meet the demands of tutors and accreditation bodies. Before you hand in your assignments, double check that you have met the requirements of your particular course or place of study.

There is guidance in each section to help you track down further information for yourself. The information in this book is by no means the end of the story. There is much more to be read, discussed and learnt from the work of the remarkable figures introduced in these pages. Check to see whether your library (either your local public library or your college or university library) can help you to track down some of the texts referred to.

Two words of warning:

Be very careful about accurate referencing. Your written work should include a clear reference to all sources that you have used in your written work, whether you have quoted directly from someone else or just referred to their ideas. Carelessness or inaccuracy could lead to you being accused of plagiarism - a very serious matter.

Secondly, use websites with caution. Some offer excellent information, others offer misleading, incomplete or sometimes simply wrong information. Always think about who published the information and when - it may be that the information is just out of date. Think too about why the person published the information. Is it someone who would like to sell you something, or would they have another motive that might prevent them telling the whole truth?

Any website addresses provided in this book were valid at the time of going to press.

Lesley Abbott

Her life

Lesley Abbott directed the national *Birth to Three Matters Project* (DfES 2002) and the follow-up *Birth to Three Training Matters Project* (Esmée Fairbairn Foundation). She has held visiting professorships at universities in Australia, Singapore and Ireland. She was a member of a committee of enquiry into educational provision for three and four year olds. This committee, chaired by Angela Rumbold, produced a report in 1990 entitled *Starting with Quality*.

Her contributions to policy, training and practice in the field of early childhood education were recognised by the award of the Order of the British Empire in 2005. She is currently Research Professor at Manchester Metropolitan University, where she has spent much of her career.

Her writing

Lesley has become best known for her work in developing *Birth to Three Matters* (DfES 2002). The aim of the pack was to provide support, information and guidance for practitioners with responsibility for the care and education of babies and children from birth to three years. It provided information on child development, effective practice, examples of activities which promote play and learning, guidance on planning and resourcing, and ways to meet diverse needs.

As well as directing the creation of the framework itself, Lesley has written a number of books arising from *Birth to Three Matters,* including *Playing to Learn: Developing High Qquality Experiences for Babies and Toddlers*, published in 2007. The year before that two books (written in conjunction with Anne Langston) were published, namely *Parents Matter: Supporting the Birth to Three Matters Framework* and *Birth to Three Matters: Supporting the Framework of Effective Practice*.

Lesley's other writing has largely focused on play and research methods with young children. In 1991, for example, she co-edited a book with Nigel Hall entitled *Play in the Primary Curriculum*. She has in addition edited a book about practice in Reggio Emilia, published in 2001 it is entitled *Experiencing Reggio Emilia – Implications for Pre-School Provision*.

Her theories and research

Lesley Abbott has worked in the field of early childhood care and education for many years. Her theory of education is intrinsic to her writing and research but rarely stated specifically. The philosophy outlined in *Starting with Quality* may be regarded as offering a guide to her views. The Rumbold Report (as it was widely known) looked at the range of provision available at that time and considered the characteristics of young learners which included:

- Variation in children's knowledge and understanding due to their different experiences
- Being active learners
- Needing first hand experiences and opportunities for exploration and play (through which children explore, apply and test out what they know and can do)
- The important role of interaction between adults and children on learning and development, and
- The changing nature of the world in which they live, which makes it difficult to foresee what they will need to know and be able to do.

In considering provision for play, Starting with Quality emphasised the need for sensitive and knowledgeable adults; careful organisation; time for children to develop their play; and observation to inform adult interventions.

A consistent thread in Lesley's theories have been around the need to protect children from over-formalisation. In *Starting with Quality* there is a specific warning that "educators should guard against pressures which might lead them to over-concentrate on formal teaching and upon the attainment of a specific set of targets". In 1999 (writing with Helen Moylett), she reiterated that view, stating that "early childhood is not a waiting room for school!"

Putting the theory into practice

Birth to Three Matters was largely aimed at a group of practitioners unused to working within a detailed framework. The fact that it was well-received by most practitioners indicates that, while the document was based on sound theories, it also offered practical advice. It was replaced in 2008 with the introduction of the Early Years Foundation Stage framework (DfES 2007).

While it was claimed that the first document had been incorporated into the earlier one, there are some aspects which perhaps make the Early Years Foundation Stage (EYFS) less practical for practitioners working with very young children. There is evidence that the four strands outlined in *Birth to Three Matters* were taken account of in developing the EYFS. There are some similarities between the strong child; the skilful communicator, the competent learner; and the healthy child proposed by *Birth to Three Matters* and the unique child; and positive relationships put forward in the EYFS. The theme of enabling environments in the EYFS clearly owes something to the earlier document.

However, the emphasis in the EYFS on the areas of learning and development has led to some practical difficulties for those working with babies and toddlers. A further comment is necessary on the shift from the strands and themes identified in *Birth to Three Matters* to the areas of learning and development identified in EYFS. The former document protected very young children by focusing on strands of development such as being a skilful communicator or a competent learner. With its emphasis on aspects such as numeracy or knowledge and understanding of the world, EYFS opened the door to approaches to teaching which could be inappropriate. This move contrasts with Abbott's long-held view on the dangers of over-formalising the curriculum for young children.

Her influence

In creating a government document such as *Birth to Three Matters*, it is sometimes necessary to steer a careful path. Abbott undoubtedly had to use a lot of influence in order to get through political opposition and to then disseminate her recommendations to a group of practitioners who had not before had to work within a detailed framework.

Comment

Although generally well received, some criticisms were levelled at *Birth to Three Matters*. Some under-threes specialists felt that Lesley Abbott was herself insufficiently expert in this field. Many believed that it placed too little emphasis on the role of key persons. This was probably due to both political and ideological pressure from those who felt that a key person might detract from the role of the parent. With the introduction of EYFS there was a much stronger emphasis on key persons - a victory for those who had continued to identify the importance of attachment, close contact and continuity between home and setting.

A further comment is necessary on the shift from the strands and themes identified in *Birth to Three Matters* to the areas of learning and development identified in EYFS. The former document protected very young children. The EYFS opened the door to approaches to teaching which could be inappropriate. This move contrasts with Abbott's long-held view on the dangers of over-formalising the curriculum for young children.

Points for reflection
- What are your views on Abbott's statement that early education is not a waiting room for school?
- Do you agree with Abbott on what is necessary to develop high quality play?

References

Birth to three matters (DfES/ Sure Start Unit 2002)
Early Years Foundation Stage (Practice Guidance) (DfES 2007)
Playing to Learn, developing high quality experiences for babies and toddlers Ann Langston and Lesley Abbott (Open University Press, 2007)
Parents Matter, Supporting the Birth to Three Matters Framework Lesley Abbott and Ann Langston (Open University Press, 2006) .
Birth to Three Matters, Supporting the Framework of Effective Practice Lesley Abbott and Ann Langston (Open University Press, 2006)
Starting with Quality (Rumbold Report) chaired by Angela Rumbold (HMSO 1990) (www.dg.dial.pipex.com/documents/docs1/rumbold.shtml)
Play in the Primary Curriculum Nigel Hall and Lesley Abbott (Hodder and Stoughton 1991)
Experiencing Reggio Emilia Lesley Abbott and Cathy Nutbrown (Open University Press 2001)
Early Education Transformed Lesley Abbott and Helen Moylett (Falmer Press 1999)

Where to find out more
'Exploring Research with Very Young Children' in A. Farrell (ed) *Exploring Ethical Research with Children* Lesley Abbott and Ann Langston (Open University Press, 2006)
'Early Childhood', in S. Fraser et al (eds) *Doing Research with Children and Young People* Ann Langston et al (Sage/ Open University Press 2004)

Jay Belsky

His life

Professor Belsky is an internationally recognized expert in the field of child development and family studies. His particular interests include the effects of day care, and parent-child relations during infancy. He is an American by birth but has lived in Britain since 2000. He is the Founding Director of the Institute of the Study of Children, Families and Social Issues, Professor of Psychology at Birkbeck College and the Research Director of the National Evaluation of Sure Start in England.

His writing

Belsky has written more than 300 articles and chapters for several books. In the 1980s and 1990s his writing included much about attachment and behavioural problems. A journal article written for *Child Development* in 2007 reflects ongoing concerns. His early raises the suggestion that:

- Poor day care is bad for very young children;
- There are ever-increasing amounts of daycare provision for babies and toddlers;
- The quality of care (at least in the United States of America, where Belsky had conducted his research) was poor;
- This has a long-term effect which, in his view, puts the nation at risk;
- Something must be done.

Belsky's more recent work has arisen directly out of his research projects and it is for these that he is perhaps best known. Of most relevance may be the National Evaluation of Sure Start published in 2007, and the findings arising from the National Institute of Child Health and Human Development (NICHD) study (www.pro-kopf.g/fileadmin/downloads/OC_37-Belsky-Effects_on_Child_Development.PDF).

His theories and research

Belsky has carried out several longitudinal and large-scale research studies. In the 1970s he became involved in the Dunedin Multidisciplinary Health and Development Project in New Zealand which continues to study a cohort of 1037 children born in 1972-3. (For further information see http://dunedinstudy.otago.ac.nz .)

He was a founding investigator on the NICHD Study of Child Care and Youth Development in the United States of America. This is a longitudinal study of the care provided for babies in 1,281 families and its impact. (For further information see www.nichd.nih.gov/research/supported/seccyd.cfm .)

Writing about the American study, Belsky comments on the difficulties of making effective judgements about mother and child relationships. In particular he suggests that the measures relating to insecure attachment are not valid. This is a common criticism of the measures (which were developed by Mary Ainsworth) and offers doubts as to whether universal conclusions can be drawn from a child's pattern of attachment. The interpretation made by researchers of children's interactions with parents may not alone indicate poor (or healthy) attachment.

In the NICHD study he highlights the anti-social and aggressive behaviour shown by some children in day care situations, where children are in day care for more than 20 hours per week(or in some reports 30 hours a week). However, the researchers found a high correlation between high quality care and better vocabulary scores - regardless of the amount of time the child had spent in child care or even the type of care.

Similar themes emerged from his evaluation of the Sure Start programme. The interim report published in 2005 was critical of the impact of the programmes, suggesting that in Sure Start areas the most disadvantaged groups had fared somewhat worse than similar groups in non-Sure Start areas. This received widespread press coverage. The report released in 2008 showed much improvement. Many highly disadvantaged families were shown to be benefiting from the programmes but press reports continued to emphasise the earlier findings. (See for example Hilary Wilce's write up in the Independent on Thursday, 8 May 2008).

Putting the theory into practice

Belsky has suggested that the findings from Sure Start programmes should lead to changes "on humanitarian grounds". He believes that tax policies should reduce - rather than increase - the pressure on parents to leave their youngsters in the care of others. This would he believes give parents the opportunity to stay at home with young children, should they wish to do so.

He also suggests that there should be an increase in paid parental leave in order to reduce the amount of time that children spend in centre-based care. He is reported in several newspapers as suggesting that "the risks are that more hours in any kind of childcare across the first four-and-a-half years of life and, independently, the more time in childcare centres, the higher the levels of problem behaviour (and) that children who spend more time in non-maternal care through their infancy, toddler and pre-school years experience somewhat less harmonious mother-child relationships through their first three years. They start school being somewhat more aggressive and disobedient than children with less non-maternal care experience".

There are other similarities between Belsky's NICHD research and The Effective Provision of Pre-School Education (EPPE) project in this country. Professor Belsky indicates that there are less damaging effects in "high-quality childcare", which should be encouraged. He goes so far as to suggest that there are clear benefits for children attending high quality provision - and that there should be expansion. His definition of quality is thought to be based on well-trained staff and good child to staff ratios.

Jay Belsky

His influence

Many people active in the field of care and education for children up to three years of age were surprised by the appointment of Jay Belsky to evaluate the Sure Start Project, since it was felt that he had demonstrated in his writing a negative view of group care for very young children. He is not alone in consistently taking the line that the quality and type of child care a child experiences early in life can have a lasting impact on their development. He clearly is influential in that he has been involved in the leadership of three highly significant and large-scale studies. It is interesting to note that in spite of the initially critical evaluation of Sure Start, the government continued to put money into the project - taking the advice of the researchers that it was too early to be evaluating such a far-reaching scheme. This hesitance paid off as the second evaluation was much more positive.

It could however also be argued that Belsky lacks influence since he has been giving much the same message for more than twenty years without any indication of a major change of direction in daycare provision - either here or in the United States. He offers the explanation that research findings can be interpreted differently and suggests that if acted on his findings might mean that affordable day care would cease to be available for the most disadvantaged parents.

Comment

It is very difficult to judge Belsky's research and theories since his findings are so much surrounded by mass hysteria about day care. Reports of the main Sure Start evaluation findings have been eclipsed by reference to the more negative interim report. Although, for example, the findings about levels of aggression in children attending group care settings have been heavily reported the fact that it applies to only 17% of the children involved is not reported. This has also to be compared to the fact that 6% of similarly aggressive children who had not spent long periods in day care.

Belsky is also open about the fact that the NICHD research has limitations. He suggests that the group of children selected for the study may not be representative of the full range within the population, since the most socially-economically deprived and other at risk groups were specifically excluded from the study. In addition, some of the poorest provision was also excluded from the research. This means that he is unable to make what he terms a 'compensatory hypothesis' - since it is difficult to know whether more needy groups would have gained more benefits. He concludes that high quality provision produces better outcomes for children but suggests that the length of time spent at nursery does not necessarily affect what is gained for the child.

This is in contrast to The Effective Provision of Pre-School Education project (EPPE), which indicates increased benefits from increased attendance. The EPPE project also differs in finding less benefit from enhanced staff ratios, however these differences are almost certainly due to the fact that EPPE focused on older children.

Points for reflection

- What are your views on the levels of aggression apparently found in children attending group care for longer periods of time?
- Why do you think there were marked differences in the findings of the interim and later Sure Start evaluations?

References

Belsky, J. (2008). '*Quality, Quantity and Type of Child Care: Effects on Child Development in the USA*'. In G. Bentley & R. Mace (Eds.), *Substitute parenting: Alloparenting in human societies*. Jay Belsky (Berghahn Books 2008)
The Child in the Family was published in 1984
'Are there long term effects of early childhood care?' *Child Development* Jay Belsky et al (March/April Vol.78 No.2 pages 681-701)

Where to find out more

www.surestart.gov.uk
Birth to Three matters: a review of the literature Tricia David et al (DfES 2007) Research Report RR444 (www.standards.dfes.gov.uk/eyfs/research/downloads/rr444.pdf)

Urie Bronfenbrenner

His life

Urie Bronfenbrenner was born in Moscow, Russia. When he was six years old his family, who were Jewish, emigrated to the United States. His father was a clinical pathologist and worked in a home for what was then termed 'the mentally retarded'. Bronfenbrenner took his first degree in psychology and music but went on to focus more specifically on developmental psychology. On completing his PhD in 1942, he served in the Army Air Corps as a psychologist. At the end of the Second World War he worked with men who had been discharged from the armed services.

In his subsequent work, his interest in development and its context was clear. In 1948 he became Professor of Human Development at the University of Michigan and at the time of his death he was Emeritus Professor of Human Development and of Psychology in the Cornell University College of Human Ecology. He had six children, some of whom have followed in his footsteps.

His writing

He was the author, co-author or editor of more than three hundred articles or chapters and fourteen books. His key themes throughout his career were the links between development and ecology. For example *Making Human Beings Human* was first published in 1971 and is described as presenting a bioecological perspective on development. This idea was followed up in 1979 with the first publication of his most famous book *The Ecology of Human Development*.

Bronfenbrenner was also interested in cross-cultural studies. *Two Worlds of Childhood* was published in 1975, and *The Twelve who Survive* in 1992 - the twelve in the title referring to the fact that around the world twelve out of thirteen babies survive birth.

His theory

Bronfenbrenner is mainly remembered for the development of his Ecological Systems Theory, which is described in *The Ecology of Human Development*. It is said that human ecology is an interdisciplinary area of learning, which Bronfenbrenner himself created.

He initially identified four systems of human ecology, presenting his model as a series of concentric circles. The inner ring he called the microsystem. It consists of the child and "the objects to which he responds or the people with whom he interacts on a face-to-face basis" (1979, page 7).

The *mesosystem* applies to the settings and links between the settings in which the child, (or 'developing person' as Bronfenbrenner describes the child), participates. These might include a place of worship, the extended family, nursery or aspects of the community.

The *exosystem* includes people and places with which the child may not directly participate or interact with, but which nonetheless affect his or her immediate environment. One example may be the place where the parent works or the class attended by a sibling. Bronfenbrenner suggests that the influence of the exosystem on the microsystem may be two-way. He gives examples of the parents of children with disabilities. The exosystem for these children may include organisations which support the rights of such children without actually coming into contact with the children themselves. In addition, what the child does or needs (such as a particular type of schooling or resource) may impact on the organisation.

The fourth ring or system, Bronfenbrenner called the *macrosystem* (or the larger socio-cultural context). Bronfenbrenner describes this in cross-cultural terms. In France, for example, schools

Urie Bronfenbrenner

and cafes and playgrounds may vary but there will be many similarities. The same can be said in the United States of America. However "in both worlds, homes, day care, day care centers, neighbourhoods, work settings, and the relations between them are not the same for well-to-do families as for the poor". It is these global similarities and 'intersocietal contrasts' to which Bronfenbrenner is referring when he writes of the macrosystem.

He later (1986) added a fifth element, called the *Chronosystem* (or the evolution of the external systems over time). The chronosystem is not represented as one of the concentric circles but is intended to show the way in which changes over time within cultures and mesosystems impact on the developing person. One example he gives is of the impact of divorce - where effects may not be felt until some time after the event and where the impact may be greater for boys than girls. In addition the impact may vary from culture to culture.

Putting the theory into practice

Throughout his career, Bronfenbrenner tried to spearhead new developments in theory and research design, which he hoped both academics and practitioners would be able to apply to their work. Bronfenbrenner is not widely recognised as helping practitioners to put his ideas into practice and this may be why someone who has done so much to change the thinking of both groups is not better known.

There are perhaps two key areas where his ideas may be seen in practice. The first is in his role as the father of Head Start. Established in 1965, Head Start was designed to support poor families in enabling children to be more successful at school. A range of pre-school programmes were developed as part of this American government initiative, of which High/Scope is by far the most well-known and most well-documented.

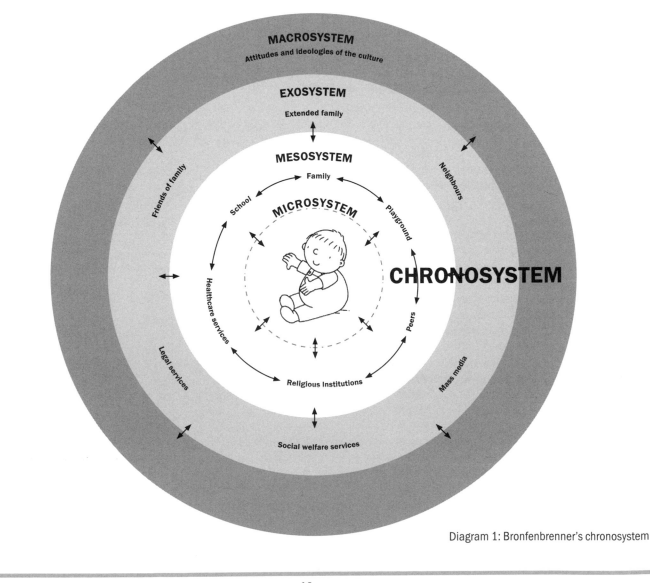

Diagram 1: Bronfenbrenner's chronosystem

The second area of work where theory can be seen in practice comes from the influence of Bronfenbrenner's groundbreaking work in "human ecology". The impact of this work is difficult to over-estimate. In part, because of his theories, academics and practitioners are much more likely to take account of children's context in considering learning and development. Development is more widely seen as a lifelong process rather than merely something confined to chidlhood. In applying Bronfenbrenner's "bioecological" theories, social scientists have been able to make connections between disciplines, and these in turn have allowed findings to emerge about which key elements in the larger social structure, and across societies, are vital for optimal human development.

His influence

His writings have been widely translated and his students and colleagues number among today's most internationally influential developmental psychologists. In 1996 Bronfenbrenner was given a lifetime award 'in the service of science and society' by the American Psychological Association. This is now known as "The Bronfenbrenner Award" and is awarded annually. In his obituary, the president of Cornell University described him "as the father of the Head Start program and a lifelong advocate for children and families". Head Start paved the way for an approach to early childhood care and education which has been highly influential. The long-term documented success of High/Scope in turn led the way for Sure Start in England and alerted politicians in general to the power of early intervention.

In his obituary in the university newssheet, it is suggested that before Bronfenbrenner, "child psychologists studied the child, sociologists examined the family, anthropologists the society, economists the economic framework of the times and political scientists the structure". The obituary continues: "as the result of Bronfenbrenner's groundbreaking concept of the ecology of human development, these environments -- from the family to economic and political structures -- are viewed as part of the life course, embracing both childhood and adulthood". The LA Times obituary added "the theory has helped tease out what is needed for the understanding of what makes human beings human", describing Bronfenbrenner as the person "whose theories profoundly altered the understanding of what children need to develop into successful adults".

Comment

While Bronfenbrenner's theory, in line with the social constructionist theories of Vygotsky, highlighted the environmental influences on development it has been criticised for placing too little emphasis on biological and cognitive factors.

Head Start led to many important changes in the way in which early childhood education was valued. However, it could be criticised for leading politicians and policy makers (and perhaps eventually practitioners) to place too much emphasis on easily measurable results and to ignore some of the more important indicators of becoming human - such as well-being and positive dispositions to learning.

Bronfenbrenner did spend many of his later years warning that the process that makes human beings human is breaking down. He wrote that in 1971 that modern lifestyles threatened the future of the country by "depriving (them) of their birthright ... virtues, such as honesty, responsibility, integrity and compassion" - evidenced in apathy and violence. In this he was ahead of many writers (see for example Gerhardt and Palmer) who also warn that there is a crisis which threatens the competence and characteristics of the next generation of adults. He suggests that "it is still possible to avoid that fate. We now know what it takes to enable families to work the magic that only they can perform. The question is, are we willing to make the sacrifices and the investment necessary to enable them to do so?" In the later edition of *Making Human Beings Human* Bronfenbrenner writes:

> *The major social changes taking place recently in modern industrial society.... may have altered environmental conditions conducive to human development to such a degree that the process of making human beings human is being placed in jeopardy.* (2004 page xxvii)

Points for reflection

- Do you agree with Bronfenbrenner's gloomy analysis of the future of humans?
- Consider the impact of Bronfenbrenner's work on multi-professional work.

References

Two Worlds of Childhood: US and USSR, Urie Bronfenbrenner (Penguin 1975)
The Ecology of Human Development: Experiments by Nature and Design. Urie Bronfenbrenner (Harvard University Press 1979)
The Twelve who Survive Urie Bronfenbrenner (Routledge 1992)
Making Human Beings Human Urie Bronfenbrenner (Sage Publications 2004) (First published 1971)

Where to find out more

Toxic Childhood Sue Palmer (Orion 2007)
Why Love Matters Sue Gerhardt (Brunner Routledge 2004)

Tina Bruce

Her life

Tina Bruce is an honorary visiting professor at Roehampton University and previously held a similar role at London Metropolitan University. She works as a consultant with local authorities and a range of early years settings. She originally trained at the Froebel Educational Institute as a primary teacher with an emphasis on children aged 3-7 years and has taught in both special and mainstream school contexts. Tina originally trained at the Froebel Educational Institute as a primary teacher (3-13 years) with an emphasis on 3-7 years. She also trained (Post Graduate Certificate in Education of the Deaf) to teach children with hearing impairments at the University of Manchester (1970-71). She was head of the Froebel Research Nursery School and gained her Masters degree at the Froebel Educational Institute.

She has worked with the British Council in New Zealand and Egypt. She was appointed to be a member of the working parties in England which developed The 'Curriculum Guidance for the Foundation Stage' (QCA/DfEE, 2000), the 'Birth to Three Matters Framework' (DfES, 2002) and the Foundation Stage Profile (QCA/DfES, 2003). She was the coordinator of the Early Years Advisory Group to successive government ministers for children for 10 years. She was made an International Woman Scholar by the University of Virginia Commonwealth in 1989. In 2009 she was awarded a CBE for her services to early childhood education in the UK.

Her writing

She has written and edited around thirty books as well as a great many articles and was resident expert for the BBC series Tuning into Children. She is founding editor of *Early Childhood Practice: the Journal for Multi-Professional Partnerships*, which is now in its tenth year.

Tina's first book was entitled *Early Childhood Education* (1987), now in its third edition (2005). She was, through the publication of this book, the first to make the notion of schema widely accessible. She has edited series of books for Hodder and Stoughton and the Open University Press. Her books *Learning Through Play* and *Cultivating Creativity* are firm favourites. *Child Care and Education* was originally published in 1996. It was originally co-written with Carolyn Meggitt and is now in its fourth edition.

Her theory

Bruce describes herself as 'a social learning theorist.... influenced by the work of Froebel'. She favours an holistic approach to teaching young children which focuses on creativity, play and first-hand experiences.

Early in her writing, Tina identified ten principles of early childhood education. These drew on pioneering philosophies including the work of Froebel, Montessori and Steiner. This was in itself a pioneering approach - showing clearly the legacy left by the earlier theorists and thinkers. The ten principles are widely quoted and include consideration of:

- A child's need to be a child;
- The holistic nature of development and the integrated nature of learning;
- The importance of opportunities to act as an independent learner, making choices and mistakes with an emphasis on self-motivation;
- Receptive learning periods - practice won't help until the brain and body are sufficiently developed;
- A focus on what children are able to do - taking that as the starting point for learning;
- Imagination and symbolic representation which support development;
- The central role of relationships with others in children's development.

The final principle highlights the essential interaction between child, context and curriculum content if education is to be successful.

A major aspect of Tina's theoretical approach to early education is based around schema. Tina Bruce was the teacher involved in Athey's seminal research in this area. Together they analysed children's representations including play. In their analysis they were able to identify a number of schema. Athey (2003) describes a schema as "a pattern of repeated actions. Clusters of schemas develop into later concepts".

Another key element of Bruce's theory is the value of what she terms 'free-flow' play. For her, children's play is at its richest when they are able to 'wallow' in it. She identifies twelve characteristics which mark this out from other forms of play. These include:

- First hand experience
- Developing rules and props
- Freely chosen activity
- Rehearsing recent learning or celebrating learning, imagining the future, pretending
- Deep involvement and 'personal play agenda'
- Co-ordinated ideas and feelings.

9. Children sometimes make play agendas or scripts. If adults want to join in they must follow the child's script and not impose their own.
10. Children 'wallow' in their feelings. A scale of involvement, developed in Belgium by Professor Ferre Laevers, enables us to decide how immersed in the situation they are. This is important as in Tina's words "concentration is the greater predictor of academic success".
11. When children play, they show their skills and competencies.
12. Finally, play helps co-ordinate and integrate what the child learns, and brings together all the different aspects of a child's development.

(www.cowgateunder5s.co.uk)

Schema theory evolved from observations of. practice. Chris Athey and Tina Bruce were able to identify situations where children's movements, drawings or constructions made clear use of particular themes. Young children, for example, often begin by making much use of vertical and horizontal marks and movements. Children described as focusing on circular schema would favour circular movements and round and round mark-making. Transporting is a schema readily recognised by all practitioners - children collecting objects from all areas of provision into bags or trucks and moving them from one place to another.

Putting the theory into practice

At a Scottish children's centre, staff have translated the twelve features of play into a form that is accessible to parents. This supports both parents and practitioners in putting theory into practice and is shown below:

The following 12 points enable play to take place.

1. Children need first-hand experiences, which need not always be fun. Tina says "children cannot play if they are sitting at tables".
2. Children make up their own rules while they play. Being in control is an important part of play.
3. Sometimes something a child has made earlier becomes a 'play prop'.
4. A child must want to play and must be in the mood.
5. Children role play and pretend to be other people.
6. Children 'pretend play' which is not necessarily rehearsing for later life.
7. Sometimes children play alone.
8. Children play in pairs, in parallel or in groups.

Tina Bruce

Of Tina's many talents it is perhaps her ability to put complex ideas into a form that makes sense to practitioners and is most admired. Her detailed observations of children at play strike a chord with practitioners enabling them to understand the links between theory and practice.

Her influence

This ability has given Tina Bruce a great deal of influence. Practitioners frequently admire the advice she gives - perhaps because it has an iconoclastic edge. Wallowing in free-flow play does not appear anywhere in the EYFS or similar documents, and yet it carries the essence of young children's joyful excitement in a world which is new to them. That enthusiasm is frequently transferred to practitioners themselves. The Block Play Research Project for example, of which Tina was director, remains an invaluable collaborative action research into the value of construction with wooden blocks.

Tina's undoubted widespread influence is all the more remarkable when her role in government thinking over the last decade is remembered. She has managed to maintain enthusiasm for developments beyond the documents which she has been instrumental in developing. The Foundation Stage Profile is a case in point.

Comment

The greatest criticism widely voiced of Bruce's work has focused around the Foundation Stage Profile. Before he died, Professor Ted Wragg frequently ridiculed the document, which required judgements on so many aspects of children's development, as unworkable and impractical.

There are also criticisms of the notion of free-flow play. Some theorists, such as Janet Moyles, favour playful teaching or a more instrumental use of play. Tina has consistently maintained that play is only play if it is self-chosen and directed. It is interesting to compare this idea with the concept of flow described by Csikszentmihalyi, the highly respected expert in the field of creativity, who uses the term 'flow' to describe the apparently effortless yet focused nature of creative people at their most creative.

Points for reflection
- If you are not familiar with schema look up some of the references suggested below.
- How can ideas of the value of play be most effectively communicated to parents?

References
Cultivating Creativity in Babies, Toddlers and Young Children Tina Bruce (Hodder and Stoughton 2004)
Early Childhood Education Tina Bruce (Hodder and Stoughton 2005/ 3rd ed)
Child Care and Education Tina Bruce and Carolyn Meggitt (Hodder Arnold 1996/ 1st ed)
Learning through Play Tina Bruce (Hodder and Stoughton 2001)

Where to find out more
Creativity, Flow and the Psychology of Discovery and Invention Mihali Csikszentmihalyi (Harper Perennial 1997)
Extending Thought in Young Children Chris Athey (Paul Chapman Publishing 2007/ 2nd ed.)

His life

During the 1970s and 1980s Guy Claxton was involved in teacher education in London. For many years he has been the Professor of the Learning Sciences at Bristol University. His writing and theories reflect his interest in lifelong learning and concern for global, environmental, political, economic and spiritual issues. His training in psychotherapy and interest in Buddhism are indicative of the wide range of interests and expertise which he brings to his writing and research.

His writing

Claxton is a prolific writer and the titles of his work often reflect his challenging views. His best-selling and perhaps best known book is *Hare Brain Tortoise Mind - why intelligence increases when you think less* which was first published in 1997. Other titles include *What's the point of school?* (2008) and *Wise up! learning to live the learning life* (1999). Claxton's writing is not always an easy read but it is rewarding and worth persevering with.

His theories

Claxton's theories have spanned many decades and are very wide-ranging. Key elements include:

Intuition - much of Claxton's earlier writing focused on the role of intuition in work with children. He describes intuition as one 'way of knowing', a common theme of his writing. He suggests that intuition involves expertise, judgment, sensitivity, creativity and rumination. These factors together contribute to practitioners' ability to reflect, which he suggests can be harnessed and developed but which will wither if neglected or ignored.

Slow ways of knowing - this is a term which Claxton coined in his book *Hare Brain Tortoise Mind*. In that book he suggests that the default mode for modern-day thinking is fast and unreflective - hare brain. He highlights the importance of allowing other ways of thinking - the tortoise mind - to thrive. He underlines, citing several research studies, the way in which too much conscious thinking and too little rumination can undermine perception and understanding. He describes a study undertaken by Jerome Singer (a well-know play theorist). Subjects were asked to select a square from range of squares in front of them that matched a square placed at some distance from them. When the same people were asked not simply to select the appropriate square but to pretend that they had bet on getting the right answer, their performance went down. In a similar study, people were asked to undertake an eye test. When asked to undertake the eye test as part of pretending to be a pilot, subjects did very much better. In each case the amount of pressure, anxiety and frustration felt by people involved in the study affected their performance.

Learnacy - Claxton has chosen this term in an ironic way - saying that he would never want to see it used in planning. He chose it to echo the undue emphasis which he believes is placed on literacy and numeracy at the expense of learning in general. He suggests that 4Rs are involved in exercising the brain:

- **Resilience** (or sticking at things) which involves curiosity, risk-taking, persistence, flexibility, being observant and focused;
- **Reflection** (or taking stock of your own learning) which involves opportunities to decide what, when and how they will go about learning, and to think about the effort they have contributed to a task or activity;
- **Reciprocity** (being able to learning alone and with others) - powerful learners, Claxton suggests, need to be able to work independently;

Guy Claxton

■ **Resourcefulness** (or being able to learn in different ways) which might include daydreaming and analysis; questions and silence; being poetic and scientific, playing, exploring and experimenting.

The building blocks of learning power - Claxton identifies eight building blocks:

■ **Curiosity** - since children are born curious the role of adults is to nurture their interest and help them to develop what Claxton calls 'healthy scepticism'.

■ **Exploration** - involves wanting to know and problem-finding but it also involves enjoyment of slow thinking or daydreaming.

■ **Courage** - being a courageous learner involves taking risks, getting things wrong and sticking at things.

■ **Experimentation** - involves getting things wrong and being prepared to take a long time to work things out.

■ **Imagination** - involves making unusual connections, and young children make more and more unusual connections than anyone else. This is an ability that should be nurtured and encouraged.

■ **Discipline** - in addition to imagination, Claxton maintains that effective learners need both imagination and the ability to plan and act rigorously.

■ **Sociability** - learning to share their ideas with others involves learning how to listen, who to listen to and when.

■ **Thoughtfulness** - Claxton believes that learning is better and more creative when we take time and give learners space. Rushing children causes them to think in a rut and can prevent them from thinking the unusual or less obvious thoughts, that are the only ones that can arise in unhurried contexts.

Creativity - Claxton has written widely on this subject and writes in a no-nonsense style about ways in which practitioners can support it. In an article on his website (see details below) he explodes a number of myths about creativity, reminding readers that creativity is not always comfortable but that it isn't wacky or solitary. It does not have one special place in the brain and is not easy to assess. He links it to 'slow ways of knowing' by reminding us that often creative ideas have to be put on a back burner and left to bubble up in our 'intelligent unconscious'.

He goes on to suggest that there are 8 'I's to creativity:

■ **Immersion** knowing a lot and having a lot of expertise in the areas in which creativity may be developed.

■ **Inquisitiveness** promoting curiosity, knowing that not all problems have an easy answer.

■ **Investigation** Claxton quotes Piaget as saying that investigation is about knowing what to do when you don't know what to do.

■ **Interaction** involves not just being with others but having time and space to share ideas and thoughts in a meaningful way.

■ **Imagination**

■ **Intuition**

■ **Intellect** Claxton reminds us that creativity is not easy or simply innate but requires thought and effort.

■ **Imitation** is not a passive or simple part of children's learning. We all, including children, learn from others. Claxton quotes Einstein as saying that the only serious method of education is to offer an example. Adults must model what they want to develop in children, including creativity.

Putting the theory into practice

Claxton writes about all phases of education and age groups but the philosophies he demonstrates in his writing apply very effectively to young children. The common themes that he highlights are in line with many other early childhood philosophies. His theories build on the key characteristics of young learners - curiosity, imagination, and exploration.

By reducing complex ideas to short phrases and individual words Claxton supports practitioners in taking on his complex ideas. Promoting the 4Rs, the 8Is or the 8 building blocks of learning may seem daunting - but perhaps taking on a single idea such as giving children the time and space they need for slow ways of knowing or encouraging them to develop a full range of sensory and physical learning approaches may be more your style!

HIs Influence

Claxton has the ability to make what are essentially esoteric and sometimes difficult ideas accessible. His work is known and used in a number of schools - not only in this country but in Australia and New Zealand. Changing the minds of politicians and policy makers is no easy matter but perhaps Claxton's influence comes from the fact that he enables practitioners to find a voice. The ideas that he proposes such as slow ways of knowing make common sense to practitioners - appeal to their intuitions which in turn arise from their knowledge of children.

Comment

Claxton's work challenges many popular and political ideas of effective education. Traditionalists and policy makers often believe that quick-fixes are needed and that the disappointing results achieved in many schools can be reversed by going 'back to basics'. This means that Claxton's messages are not always welcomed by politicians and officials who believe that tighter targets are all that is needed to improve learning. It is all too easy to make ideas, such as Building Learning Power or 'slow ways of knowing', sound woolly - but that does not mean that they are without substance or value.

A second criticism is of a rather different nature. It comes from those who support Claxton's ideas, but who dislike the way they are marketed to draw in business interests. For this group of critics Claxton's work can feel like a sell-out, as they believe that important educational ideas such as this should be free from financial motives. If asked, Claxton might maintain that this is a valid and effective way to get important messages across to influential people who need to hear and understand what he has to say about children, schools and learning. The personal integrity reflected in so much of Claxton's writing suggests that this may be the case.

Claxton, in common with Howard Gardner and Susan Greenfield, is critical of the current focus on learning styles. He suggests that the acronym for Visual-Auditory-Kinaesthetic learning (VAK) actually stands for vacuous! Gardner, Claxton and Greenfield all indicate that different learning situations demand different learning approaches and that all human learning involves the merging of different sensory inputs. This is particularly relevant to practitioners working with very young children who need to develop a wide range of approaches to learning since, in the foundation stage, they are laying foundations of all later learning in the brain. All young children are and should be encouraged to be 'kinaesthetic' learners. Effective learning at this stage must involve physical action as well as exploration of texture, shape and form. In addition, children must be developing ways of seeing and hearing that inform all of their learning.

Points for reflection
- Why has the focus on learning styles achieved such popularity when it appears to have no scientific basis?
- How can you promote slow ways of knowing?

References
www.buildinglearningpower.co.uk
Hare Brain Tortoise Mind Guy Claxton (Basic Books 1997)
Wise up! Learning to Live the Learning Life Guy Claxton (Bloomsbury Network Press 1999)
What's the point of school? Guy Claxton (One World Publications 2008)

Where to find out more
www.guyclaxton.com
Creativity, Wisdom and Trusteeship Anna Craft et al (eds) (Harvard Business School Press 2008)
The Intuitive Practitioner Terry Atkinson and Guy Claxton (eds) (Open University Press 2000) (see chapter 2)

Edward de Bono

PROFILE

de Bono has been described as a polymath - good at everything. It was he who introduced the term 'lateral thinking' and over many years he has gone on to develop thinking about creativity in the world of both business and education.

KEY DATES

1933   Born in Malta

LINKS

- *How Children Learn 2*
  Theories about creativity

His life

Edward do Bono was born in Malta. Although he took his first degree there and achieved a medical qualification, he won a scholarship and subsequently went on to study at Oxford University. He has achieved several doctorates at Oxford, Cambridge and in Malta and has worked at Oxford, Cambridge, London and Harvard Universities. He describes his work as having world-wide implications and indeed he has lectured in over fifty countries.

His writing

He has written numerous books which have been translated into over thirty languages, including Hebrew, Arabic, Bahasa, Urdu, Slovene and Turkish. de Bono's earliest books (written in the 1960s and 1970s) had titles such as *The Five Day Course in Thinking; Teaching Thinking and Practical Thinking*. Since that time the theme has remained the same but the titles have become more upbeat - *Creativity Workout and Six Thinking Hats*.

His theories and thinking

His theories have three key elements:

Problem-solving which is defined as finding the problem and ways to fix it
Creative problem-solving which requires finding new ways to fix things, and
Lateral thinking - a term it is claimed that he devised. This is defined as having a tool kit or method to support both problem solving and creative problem solving processes in devising solutions.

The theory on which *Six Thinking Hats* is based asks the reader (or learner) to consider a toolkit of six ways of thinking. The descriptions below highlight the kinds of thinking which de Bono suggests support lateral thinking, creative problem-solving and everyday problem-solving.

White Hat: encourages you first to look at the information you have, and see what you can learn from it.
Red Hat: encourages the wearer to look at the situation intuitively exploring emotions and feelings - not just yours but the possible reactions of others affected.
Black Hat: should lead the thinker to look at the issue under consideration pessimistically, trying to identify what could go wrong.
Yellow Hat: contrary to the black hat this hat leads you to think positively - seeing opportunities and benefits
Green Hat: using the green hat should help to develop creative solutions to a problem. Criticisms do not belong in this category as it should be open-ended.
Blue Hat: this hat is worn by the person managing the process. If more ideas are needed he or she may request more green hat thinking or yellow hat thinking if there are too many negative ideas around. This hat should also encourage everyone involved to be aware of the overall process - are some people talking too much; is too much time being spent on a particular focus and so on.

This gives a flavour of de Bono's extensive work. His theories are concerned with finding ways to support creative and effective thinking.

Putting the theory into practice

Edward do Bono's work has been developed and applied in business, industry and education around the world. You have only to look at his website to get some idea of the extent to which his theories are applied in many walks of life. His website indicates that his books and approaches are used in the University of Buenos Aires. In Venezuela, all children are required to spend an hour a week on his programmes. It is claimed that thousands of schools in Asia, the U.S.A., Canada, Australia, New Zealand, Ireland and the UK are using de Bono's programmes for the teaching of thinking.

Although a great deal has been done in schools, the theories are not generally applied to work with very young children. In 1992 he first published *Teach Your Child How to Think* and in that he writes about eight year olds but that appears to be the lower limit of his work. His concern for children's thinking is reflected in his words "perhaps the most important benefit from teaching thinking is the increase in self esteem and self confidence of those taught. A youngster taught thinking feels in control of his or her life – instead of feeling like a cork carried along by the stream of life and controlled by the currents" (www.makingthinkingmatter.org). However, an organisation called Capture Arts have attempted to apply de Bono's work to work in pre-schools. They train practitioners to work with children in ways which encourage the use of all six modes of thinking in developing creative structures.

His influence

de Bono's website suggests that he "is one of the very few people in history who can be said to have had a major impact on the way we think. In many ways he could be said to be the best known thinker internationally." He lectures around the world and has received awards which mark him out as a pioneer in this field.

His work has had a high profile over several decades and shows no sign of losing popularity. Books written almost forty years ago continue to sell. Training courses continue to be run. It is difficult to assess the reasons for such popularity but the accessibility of his thinking and writing is a factor.

Comment

There are three possible areas of criticism of what is undoubtedly highly successful work. The first involves the nature of the business. Training courses are expensive and therefore limited to small numbers of people. Does this sit comfortably with someone who claims to be working for the good of humankind?

Secondly, some educationalists feel that teaching thinking in isolation is inappropriate. They would prefer that thinking skills are developed in the course of other learning. They feel that de Bono's approaches are too formalised and system-led.

Thirdly, de Bono gives little or no evidence base for his work. This means that others cannot follow-up his ideas with clear reference to the theoretical or philosophical underpinning.

Points for reflection
- Do you think that thinking skills have a place in work with very young children?
- Why do you think de Bono's work has maintained such popularity over so many decades?

References
Six Thinking Hats Edward de Bono. (Pelican 1987)
Five day course in thinking Edward de Bono (Penguin 1967)
Teaching thinking Edward de Bono (Penguin 1976)
Practical Thinking Edward de Bono (Penguin 1971)
Creativity Workout Edward de Bono (Penguin 2008)
Teach your Child how to think Edward de Bono (Penguin 1992)

Where to find out more
www.edwarddebono.com
New thinking: the use of lateral thinking, Edward do Bono (Jonathan Cape 1967)
Capture Arts www.makingthinkingmatter.org

Mary-Jane Drummond

Her life

Mary Jane Drummond works in the School of Education at the University of Cambridge. She started teaching in an infants school in London's East End in 1966 and since then has taught in a variety of inner-city schools; she was the head teacher of a school in Sheffield for four years. In the 1970s, she worked at the University of Leeds on the Schools Council Project Communication Skills in Early Childhood. In 1985, she joined the Institute of Education in Cambridge, which was incorporated into the University of Cambridge in 1992. She has close links with the Early Childhood Unit at the National Children's Bureau and with them has published in-service development packs of materials for early years educators.

Her writing

Mary-Jane Drummond's best-known book is *Assessing Children's Learning* which was first published by David Fulton in 1993 and which remains a well-respected book. She has written a wealth of other material - often as chapters in other people's books or as joint ventures. As an example of the first, we might consider a chapter entitled "Susan Isaacs—Pioneering Work in Understanding Children's Lives" in a book edited by Hilton & Hirsch which is called *Practical Visionaries: Women, Education and Social Progress* 1790–1930. Much of Drummond's writing has an historical slant. She is able to draw on the traditions of early childhood education and integrate the views and philosophies with a range of other aspects of education such as children's literature and psychoanalytic theory.

Her writing with other researchers has taken many forms. *Learning Without Limits* (published in 2004) is an example of the collaborative approach she favours. It does not focus on early years provision but offers an analysis of nine case studies of practice from year 1 to year 11. The practitioners involved all based their teaching on a concept she calls 'transformability'. The authors write about the teachers that they were:

Convinced that their priority is always to work out what they themselves can do to enable young people to become more and more powerful and committed learners. Whatever young peoples' present attainments and characteristics in performing classroom tasks, the teachers maintain an unshakeable belief in everybody's capacity to learn, and are convinced that, given the right conditions, everybody's capacity for learning can be increased and enhanced. (page 246)

She has also undertaken a range of evaluations. One of these was an evaluation of reception class provision for the Association of Teachers and Lecturers in 2005 in conjunction with Janet Moyles and others. It would be difficult to list all of Mary-Jane Drummonds publications - they pop up all over the place. It would be easy to say that this reflected her wide interests. It certainly reflects her wide knowledge but her interests are quite singular. In a chapter entitled 'Whatever Next: Future trends in early years education', Drummond highlights her passion for understanding learning:

Future developments will spring from efforts of educators who prioritise the serious work of thinking for themselves about children's learning, and thereby achieve an enhanced understanding of children and childhood.

Her theory

It is clear that at the heart of Mary-Jane Drummond's theory is her 'confident belief in children's powers' ('Children Yesterday, Today and Tomorrow' 2001 page 91). She draws on the work of many, many theorists to highlight her belief and to support her arguments. She cites the work of practitioners in Reggio Emilia - highlighting their focus on the 'hundred languages of children' and creates links with the work of Erich Fromm who wrote about the 'forgotten languages'. She quotes from Vivian Gussin Paley and from Mary Warnock in considering, from two very different perspectives, an equally respectful view of the role of imagination in learning. In writing about Steiner education (Perceptions of Play 1999 page 59), Drummond further outlines her views of play:

In play..... Children think and feel and act in ways of the utmost importance for their learning.....As long as children play, and as long as we, their educators, watch them and try to understand what we see, we will go on finding fresh ways to think about and explain the importance of play.

Putting the theory into practice

Arguably, Drummond's most powerful gift to practice is her insistence on the need for educators not only to look at children but to see and to learn from our observations. In an article entitled 'Professional Amnesia: A Suitable Case for Treatment' she reminds practitioners that 'professional knowledge exists outside ring binders' and that before the advent of frameworks and curriculum guidance 'we did know some very important things'. She draws on an eclectic range of theorists to highlight the fact that 'children's most urgent need is freedom to grow and think'. She urges practitioners to undertake some genuine reflection - critical remembering as well as critical thinking.

Her influence

This is difficult to quantify but the fact that Mary Jane Drummond, unlike many other contemporary theorists and thinkers has remained unwaveringly on the side of children must provide a constant reminder of the need to keep the learner at the centre of our thinking. Reflective practitioners would do well to read some of her writing since she has done much to keep alive the traditions and pioneering understandings of young learners. In an article in the Times Educational Supplement in 1996, which was called 'Thinking About Thinking', Mary-Jane Drummond reminded educators that they should 'spend as much time thinking about learning as thinking about teaching'. She added that 'we can't do without Piaget and all those giants'. In our reflections as educators, we can learn from reflective thinkers and theorists of earlier times.

Comment

It is difficult to be critical of Drummond's work since it is so consistent and principled. She writes admiringly of some Steiner practice but says:

I am not a Steiner educator, nor will ever be. I have no intention of settling and putting down roots within the Steiner community of discourse.

Perhaps would-be critics feel the same about Mary-Jane Drummond's philosophy. You don't have to agree or share the same sentiments to recognise its strength and honesty.

Points for reflection
- What do you think practitioners gain from "Piaget and all those giants"?

References
'Perception of Play' Mary-Jane Drummond In *Transforming Early Education* Abbott and Moylett (eds) (Falmer Press 1999)
Assessing Children's Learning Mary-Jane Drummond (David Fulton 1993/ 1st ed)
Learning without limits Susan Hart et al (Open University Press 1994)

Where to find out more
"Susan Isaacs—Pioneering Work in Understanding Children's Lives" In *Practical Visionaries: Women, Education and Social Progress* 1790–1930 Hilton & Hirsch (eds) (Longman, 2000)
"A Light in the Darkness—George MacDonald's Stories for Children" in G. Cliff Hodges, M. J. Drummond, & M. Styles (Eds.), *Tales, Tellers and Texts* (Cassell, 2000).

Judy Dunn

Her life

Judy Dunn is a Research Professor at the Institute of Psychiatry in London. She is a developmental psychologist, and has undertaken a vast range of research on children's close relationships, including siblings and friends. Most recently she has been focusing on family transitions and the impact of family change, at Cambridge University, Pennsylvania State University and the University of London. A particular interest is children's perspectives on family transitions and family processes more generally.

Among numerous honours she has received the Award for Distinguished Scientific Contributions to Child Development from the Society for Research in Child Development, and recently the G. Stanley Hall Award for Distinguished Contribution to Developmental Psychology. She is a Fellow of the British Academy and the Academy of Medical Sciences. She was a Fellow of King's College, Cambridge and is currently a Fellow of King's College, London.

Her writing

Judy Dunn has been writing in her chosen field since the 1970s and has published 18 books and over 200 papers. In 1977 she published a book entitled *Distress and Comfort*. *Sisters and Brothers* was published in 1984 and in 1988 *The Beginnings of Social Understanding*, arguably her best-known book, was published for the first time. Throughout the 1990s and into the twenty-first century, her books have focussed on sibling relationships, changing families and friendships. *Children's Friendships* (published in 2004) has also been an influential book.

Mother Care, Other Care: The British Dilemma published in 1987 was written very much in the spirit of the time when there were widespread concerns about the low levels of provision for young children. She wrote, together with Sandra Scarr, from both a personal and professional point of view. She writes of the myths that confound parents - almost as true now as when she wrote it more than twenty years ago:

Our myths about parenthood and child care defeat our unity. Mothers should stay at home with their children, yes? Good fathers should provide single-handedly for the financial needs of their wives and children, yes? Families have the responsibility to provide care for their children, as long as they are under five, yes? These are myths that did not fit the nineteenth century well, and are grotesquely out of key now....Today's image of the perfect mother who is there at the kitchen table organizing her children's play, while cooking a gourmet meal and - somehow - also succeeding at professional life, is another myth, one that's guaranteed to fill anyone who attempts to live up to it with despair, unless she has great resources of financial, practical and emotional support. (page 219)

Given this background of interest in families, as well as children's emotional and social development it is no surprise that Judy Dunn was asked to chair the Good Childhood Inquiry. She, together with Richard Layard, a professor of economics, have written up the findings of the committee, under the title of *A Good Childhood*.

Her theory

Key elements of Dunn's theories hinge around the importance of sibling relationships which teach children about managing social relationships in a context where intimacy and affection make it possible to try out unsuccessful strategies safely. A chapter written in 2008 highlights some important elements of Dunn's theories. She draws attention to aspects of young children's behaviour through which they develop social understanding. These include:

A push to make things happen by:

- Teasing - laughing and joking are excellent ways to get other people on board, and diverting conflict;
- Getting attention
- Co-operating with others in their exciting pretend play
- Subverting attention when for example siblings threaten to hog the limelight.
- Recognising that conversation supports social understanding but that "it is not solely talk about minds and feelings, it is who you talk with and why you do so that matters - and this has to do with the quality of close relationships"
- Emotion is central to close relationships and to children's curiosity about other people;
- For children to be able to construct coherent explanations of their own and others' lives they need to understand how emotion, thoughts and actions are linked over time
- Cultural understandings are grasped through close relationships.

Putting the theory into practice

In chairing the Good Childhood Inquiry, Dunn has had to draw together a wide range of views. The main recommendations (or theory into practice) are listed below (for more information see www.childrenssociety.org.uk).

The authors suggest that in order to improve the quality of children's lives;

Parents should:
- Make a long-term commitment to each other.
- Be fully informed about what is involved before their child is born.
- Love their children, each other and establish boundaries for children.
- Help children develop spiritual qualities.

Teachers should:
- Help children to develop happy, likeable social personalities.
- Base discipline on mutual respect.
- Eliminate physical and psychological violence from school.
- Make Personal, Social and Health Education statutory.
- Present sex and relationships education not as biology, but as part of social and emotional learning.
- Pilot new tests on emotional and behavioural well-being.

Government should:
- Introduce non-religious, free civil birth ceremonies.
- Offer high quality parenting classes, psychological support and adolescent mental health services throughout the country.
- Train at least 1,000 more highly qualified psychological therapists over the next five years.
- Automatically assess the mental health of children entering local authority care or custody.
- Raise the pay and status of all people who work with children including teachers and child care workers.
- Give a salary supplement to teachers taking jobs in deprived areas.
- Replace all SATS tests with an annual assessment designed mainly to guide a child's learning.
- Stop publishing data on individual schools from which league tables are constructed by the media.
- Start a major campaign to persuade employers to offer apprenticeships.
- Build a high quality youth centre for every 5,000 young people.
- Ban all building on sports fields and open spaces where children play.
- Ban firms from advertising to British children under 12.
- Ban adverts for alcohol or unhealthy food on television before 9 pm.
- Reduce the proportion of children in relative poverty from 22% to under 10% by 2015.

The media should:
- Rethink the amount of violence they put out, the unbalanced impression they give of the risks that children face from strangers and the exaggerated picture they portray of young people threatening our social stability.

Advertisers should:
- Stop encouraging premature sexualisation, heavy drinking and overeating.

All Society should:
- Take a more positive attitude to children. Welcome them into society and help them.

Judy Dunn

Her influence

As with so many contemporary theorists it is difficult to know precisely what Dunn's influence is or will become. She is however an important voice amongst those who believe that children must be not only respected but supported. She has over many years offered a consistent message which is about the importance of close relationships. In common, with many other developmental psychologists, she emphasises the interaction of nature and nurture but at the same time reminds us of the vital importance of human interaction and relationships. She presents children as lively and vigorous. In her writing on antisocial behaviour she puts forward the view that 'behavioural regulation' is what is important. Adults have to help children manage behaviour - what we do matters to who children become.

Comment

A Good Childhood, like other publications which question the world in which children are being brought up, is not without critics. Sue Palmer's book A Toxic Childhood and Susan Greenfield's concerns about the use of technology have been similarly criticised for scare-mongering and not keeping up with the times. However, Dunn joins other theorists in raising doubts about current child-rearing practices. Critics point out that throughout history there have been such concerns, but that does not mean that we should not strive to for a better future.

Points for reflection

■ Do you feel that children today have a better or worse childhood than earlier generations? Is it good enough?

References

'Relationships and Children's Discovery of the Mind' Judy Dunn in Social Life and Social Knowledge Ulrich Muller et al (eds) (Psychology Press 2008)
Distress and Comfort Judy Dunn, J. (Open Books/Fontana 1977)
Sisters and Brothers. Judy Dunn, (Fontana 1984).
Mother Care, Other Care: The British Dilemma Sandra Scarr, S., & Judy Dunn, (Penguin The Beginnings of Social Understanding Judy Dunn, (Harvard University Press.1988).
Children's Friendships: The Beginnings of Intimacy. Judy Dunn, (Blackwell publishers 2004).
A Good Childhood: Searching for Values in a Competitive Age Richard Layard and Judy Dunn (Penguin 2009)

Where to find out more
www.childrenssociety.org.uk

Carol Dweck

Her life

Carol Dweck is an American whose early study was at Columbia University. She completed her PhD at Yale University and is currently Professor of Psychology at Stanford University. She is a social psychologist and describes herself as primarily a researcher.

Her writing

Although her best-known early writing is mostly in the form of journal articles and academic papers, her most widely publicised writing is a book entitled *Mindset: The New Psychology of Success*. The Stanford University news-sheet writes that this work was based on "decades of research on achievement and success.....She makes clear why praising intelligence and ability doesn't foster self-esteem and lead to accomplishment, but may actually jeopardize success. With the right mindset...Dweck reveals what all great parents, teachers, CEOs, and athletes already know: how a simple idea about the brain can create a love of learning and a resilience that is the basis of great accomplishment in every area."

One book of particular value to early years practitioners is entitled *Self-Theories: Their Role in Motivation, Personality and Development*. The writing is clear and has plenty of examples. The message throughout is that we support children's learning best by encouraging persistence and a can-do approach.

Her theory

In the 1970s Carol Dweck's work first became well-known because of a number of articles she wrote about 'learned helplessness'. These were of particular interest at that time because of the gender slant she placed on her work. Her work showed that not only were girls more likely to show learned helplessness than boys but teachers were more likely to put boys' failures down to lack of interest or bad behaviour while any failures in girls were attributed to their lack of ability. Girls' achievements were often undermined by being said to be simply a result of hard work.

Carol Dweck's work is based on both social and developmental psychology. She focuses on the self-conceptions people use to shape their own behaviour. She looks at the origins of these self-conceptions, their role in motivation and self-regulation, and their impact on achievement and interpersonal processes. Although much of her work is concerned with intelligence she makes no attempt to define intelligence. Her research interest is in how people's implicit theories about intelligence can mould their behaviour. She suggests (2000 based on pages 1-2) that her research challenges common beliefs:

- Students with high ability are more likely to display mastery-oriented qualities - *but actually* many of these students are the most worried about failure
- Success in school fosters mastery-oriented qualities *but actually*, for children who are successful in school, success does not always boost their ability to cope with setbacks - quite the reverse
- Praise encourages mastery-oriented qualities *but actually* praising cleverness can lead to fear of failure, risk avoidance and self-doubt
- Confidence in intelligence is the key to mastery-oriented qualities *but actually* many apparently highly confident individuals are shaken when confronted with difficulty

In her book *Self-theories*, Dweck describes children who suffer from learned helplessness (who she suggests make up about half of all children) as believing that "once failure occurs, the situation is out of control and nothing can be done". Moreover, whenever children with learned helplessness meet failure they, characteristically, blame their lack of intelligence, and become less persistent and more negative. They'd say that they were not very clever; didn't have a good memory or were just not very good at tasks like the ones they were being given. Strikingly they under-estimated the number of successful tasks completed in the experiment and over-estimated the number of failures.

Dweck compares this group to another group that she terms the 'mastery-oriented'. She describes the actions of some of the group who faced with difficult challenges would say things like:

- The harder it gets, the harder I need to try;
- Mistakes are our friends;
- I love a challenge.

Although to British ears these children may sound a bit too good to be true, Dweck has no doubt that their attitudes prevented them from seeing themselves as failures. This enabled them to take risks, to persevere and to improve their performance.

'Self-theories' is another key term in Dweck's thinking. She believes that the view we hold of ourselves shapes the way we perform. If we believe that we can develop our cognitive ability we will perform. If however we think of cognitive ability as something we're born with that cannot be changed they do not persevere in difficult tasks. In this frame of thought, working hard at something implies that you are not clever (or in American terms, smart). People with this mindset also fail to take pleasure from achieving something through sustained effort.

Chen (www.edutopia.org) has summarised Dweck's theories as follows. She has, he suggests:

- "Identified two implicit theories of intelligence: Students who have an "entity" theory view their intelligence as an unchangeable internal characteristic. Students with an "incremental" theory believe that their intelligence is malleable and can be increased through effort.
- Demonstrated empirically that students who hold an entity theory of intelligence are less likely to attempt challenging tasks and are at risk for academic underachievement
- Provided evidence that praising students for their intelligence has the potential to limit their intellectual growth."

Putting the theory into practice

Dweck herself believes that mindset has an effect across all fields and uses case histories from industry, sports and the arts. In 2007, together with Ross Bentley, a world-renowned car racing coach based in Seattle, Dweck undertook a study of racing-car drivers. They wanted to see the effects of learning how to apply a growth mindset approach to their driving.

In 2007, Dweck (with two others) published a study called "Implicit Theories of Intelligence Predict Achievement Across Adolescent Transition: A Longitudinal Study and an Intervention." which showed that children with a fixed mindset about their potential could be helped to improve. She describes the fact that the group selected had over the previous two years been steadily falling behind fellow pupils who formed a control group for the experiment.

Over two years, she said, students with a fixed mindset experienced a downward academic trend while the others moved ahead. Chen (writing for the Stanford University news-sheet) describes what happened:

- The psychologists then designed an eight-week intervention program that taught some students study skills and how they could learn to be smart—describing the brain as a muscle that became stronger the more it was used. A control group also learned study skills but were not taught Dweck's expandable theory of intelligence. In just two months, she said, the students from the first group, compared to the control group, showed marked improvement in grades and study habits.
- "What was important was the motivation," Dweck said. "The students were energized by the idea that they could have an impact on their mind." Dweck recalled a young boy who was a ringleader of the troublemakers. "When we started teaching this idea about the mind being malleable, he looked up with tears in his eyes, and he said, 'You mean, I don't have to be dumb?'" she said. "A fire was lit under him."

The publication of Dweck's book *Mindset* and the research involving adolescent students has led to an approach which involves teaching children about the brain. The approach is called Brainology. It focuses on how children can be taught to "feed their own brains" through understanding that brains and cognitive development can be grown and how this mind-set can improve achievement levels. Dweck suggests that teachers and parents can help by:

- teaching children to think of their brain as a muscle that strengthens with use, and to visualize the brain forming new connections as they learn.
- teaching study skills and helping children to understand how they will help learning
- discourage labels such as "smart," or "dumb," and so on because they give the mistaken idea that IQ is fixed (see *How Children Learn 2* pages 32-44)
- praising effort rather than intelligence, and commenting on strategies and progress. If you praise intelligence it can lead children to feel stupid if they don't succeed.
- teaching children that challenging activities are fun and that mistakes are part of learning

Dweck suggests that adults working with children need to reflect on whether they themselves have fixed or growth mindsets. They should also ensure that they motivate all learners through their enthusiasm. Where teachers gave extra time to children who were struggling and asked for help, this had beneficial effects.

Her influence

Carol Dweck is not a high profile researcher and yet her theories are widely known and generally well-received. This is probably because they make human sense to us. We can identify with the situations she describes. We have experienced these feelings ourselves and know people who respond in different ways to challenging situations. Her emphasis on mastery and helplessness have meaning for many of us. The strategies she proposes are not complex and can easily be undertaken and this too contributes to the influence she is able to have.

Comment

There are perhaps two possible sources of criticism. The first lies in the marketing of Brainology. It would be all too easy for this material to fall into the category of brain tips criticised by Claxton. It is also possible that in marketing a product, the researcher's independence is lost and their research loses credibility.

The second area of possible criticism could come from those who do not share Dweck's views about the nature of Intelligence. This may include the commercial interests of companies that print and sell standard intelligence tests.

Points for reflection
■　Although much of her work is with older children it is easy to see how unhelpful mindsets can be established early in life. What can you do to ensure that this does not happen?

References
"Implicit Theories of Intelligence Predict Achievement Across Adolescent Transition: A Longitudinal Study and an Intervention." Carol Dweck et al (*Child Development* Jan/Feb 2007 78(1)246-263)
Mindset: The New Psychology of Success, Carol Dweck (Ballantine Books 2008)
Self-theories: Their Role in Motivation, Personality and Development. Carol Dweck (Psychology Press 2000)
www.edutopia.org/tell-students-feed-their-brain
http://news.stanford.ed/news/2007/february7/dweck-020707.html

Where to find out more
www.psychology.stanford.edu/~dweck

Martin Hughes

His life

Martin Hughes has worked at the University of Exeter as a Professor of Education for some years. He has researched and written on many aspects of children's learning. In recent years there has been a particular focus on children learning mathematics and the relationship between home and school, and in particular homework. However, in Martin's earlier career, he worked with Margaret Donaldson focusing on research which challenged Piaget's work. In the 1980s he worked with Barbara Tizard on the development of language at home and at nursery school.

His writing

Much of his early writing such as the studies referred to in Margaret Donaldson's book *Children's Minds*, was in the form of research papers. Throughout his career the pattern has generally been that he writes in collaboration with others. Two books, both of which have contributed a great deal to theory and practice in early childhood education, stand out. *Children and Number* (written solely by Hughes in 1986, but with a foreword by Margaret Donaldson) was subtitled *difficulties in learning mathematics*. It is regarded as important because it highlighted the problems which face children in learning mathematics and pointed to some of the aspects of the teaching of the subject which needed to be reviewed.

Young Children Learning, written in conjunction with Barbara Tizard in 1984, was considered quite controversial at the time of publication because it challenged many ideas, then current, about the development of spoken language. (For further information see pages 82-83 of *How Children Learn 2* which sets out in more detail what made this book controversial.) The language used by girls at home and at nursery school was the focus of the study. The subjects of the

research were thirty girls - fifteen of whom were described as being working class and fifteen of whom were described as middle class. All of them attended nursery school. Their talk at home (mainly with their mothers) and their talk at school was compared. Tizard and Hughes concluded that the idea that working class language was less rich than that of middle class families was a myth. They also concluded that the staffing ratios and the emphasis on play in the school did not support the girls' language development as effectively as the conversations in which they were engaged at home.

Children and Number brought to light the fact that the teaching of mathematics often failed to support learning. Hughes suggests that within early education a number of factors need to be addressed. These include:

- Stronger links between introducing the formal aspects of mathematics and children's need for concrete mathematical experience;
- Better knowledge and understanding of children's mathematical experiences is needed. Practitioners should ask themselves, for example, what children need to know about maths in their everyday lives?
- Recognising and building on the informal (and often untaught) strategies for solving mathematical problems which children already have when they start school;
- Respecting the invented symbols and ways of calculating which children often devise before they are introduced to formal mathematics;
- The use of games rather than sums;
- Using technology to help children's understanding; and
- Exploring a full range of teaching strategies.

His theories

Amongst the many varied writing and research projects in which Hughes has been involved it is possible to draw out some common threads. These could be said to form the basis of his theories about children's learning:

Constructivist views - as Margaret Donaldson's close association with Martin Hughes would suggest, his theories are constructivist. Hughes' studies used in *Children's Minds* include a well-known challenge to Piaget's three mountain test (see page 37 of *How Children Learn 1*). He devised a test which involved a small boy hiding from a policeman. Far more young children were able to solve this problem than had been the case in Piaget's original test. Donaldson suggests that this is because Hughes' test makes human sense to children - they can create a story or motive that makes sense to them in a way that they could not in the situation presented to them by Piaget. Piaget and Hughes agree that children are constructing knowledge - the difference is that Hughes (along with other post-Piagetian thinkers) stresses the importance of human feeling.

The social construction of knowledge - Hughes' theories place a strong emphasis on the role of home and parents in learning. In this he owes much to the social constructivist theories of Vygotsky (see *How Children Learn 1* page 39). He also echoes the views of Barbara Rogoff (see page 57 of this book). One major difference between Rogoff and Hughes lies in the fact that Rogoff focuses on social and creative aspects of development while Hughes researches mainly the role of parents in literacy and numeracy.

Challenging current thinking - although *Children and Number* and *Young Children Learning* focus on different aspects of development and learning, what they have in common is that they challenged current thinking about what was happening in schools at the time when they were published. A particularly striking feature of *Young Children Learning* is the way in which it challenges the idea that middle class homes and nursery schools offer a richer language learning context than the homes of working class children. Hughes' current work on homework challenges the assumption that it is of itself a good thing.

Respect for children's thinking and learning - Hughes concludes *Children and Number* by commenting on children's "immense capacity.... to grasp difficult ideas if they are presented in ways which interest them and make sense to them" (page 184).

Putting the theory into practice

Hughes' thinking and research has consistently been both challenging to practitioners and perhaps policy makers but in line with that of other theorists of his time. In the 1970s he was challenging Piagetian theories which were having a strong influence on practice. In the first half of the 1980s he was instrumental in encouraging practitioners to rethink their views on class and language. By the second half of the 1980s his research had shifted to the area of mathematics but the need for learning to make human sense to children was a theme that persisted.

Since that time there has been a major shift in mathematics teaching and learning. Practitioners have worked hard at becoming more aware of the strategies and forms of representation which children develop and use as they try to make sense of the world of number, calculation and shape, space and measures. There is much greater understanding of the need to bridge concrete and abstract aspects of mathematics (Pound 2006) and a recognition that experience alone (while essential) will not enable children to deal with abstract problems. Practitioners have become more aware of the insights to be gained from knowing about children's experiences at homes. Gifford (2006) describes some of the many aspects of mathematical learning which children gain from their home experiences including learning about money from poker sessions; about speed and distance from making many car journeys or keeping racing pigeons or understanding weights from attending a slimming club with mum! Hughes' theories have undoubtedly led many practitioners to develop more playful teaching methods with a greater emphasis on the language of mathematics.

His influence

When compared to the work of some of the other thinkers and theorists detailed in this book, Hughes' work looks quite slim. However, he has had a significant influence in broadening the understanding of practitioners and researchers in the field of early childhood. The criticisms which he and Tizard made of the support given to language development in nursery schools was in tune made by Bruner and others (including Kathy Sylva: see page 54 of this book) working on the Oxford Pre-school Research Project. Moreover, they showed some similarities to the findings of language researchers at the time - most notably Gordon Wells (see page 60 of this book).

It is perhaps in relation to mathematics that most influence can be seen. His work encouraging practitioners to look for and build on children's mathematical strategies and understanding was ahead of its time. It undoubtedly influenced the way in which the Numeracy Strategy for primary schools was set up in England and its impact can be seen in the writing of a number of early years specialists writing about mathematics twenty years later (see for example Gifford 2005; Worthington and Carruthers 2006; Pound 2006).

Comment

As can be clearly seen, Hughes' work has influenced both practitioners and theorists. Perhaps the greatest criticism has been directed at the findings presented in *Young Children Learning*. Tizard and Hughes were widely criticised for generalising their findings from a small group of girls and making sweeping assertions on the basis of those findings. They claimed for example that children use language at its most effective in situations where they are talking about everyday events. This is in contrast to the findings of Gordon Wells (see page xx of this book) who claimed that boys (as opposed to the girls in Hughes' study) used language most effectively in imaginative play situations.

There have also been criticisms of the assertion that nursery schools were unnecessarily expensive and placed too much emphasis on play. At the time of publication, the book was reviewed in all the popular press - not the usual kind of review for newspapers such as the Sun or Mirror. In their foreword the authors suggest that their work should not be taken as a criticism of nursery education but inevitably it was widely seen as such. Subsequently however, their suggestions that nurseries and playgroups should build more on children's previous knowledge and experience has had an impact on practice. Their idea that children need to get out into the world beyond nursery is also an important aspect of many early years settings.

Points for Reflection
- Where and when do you think children use language most effectively? Is it different for boys and girls?

References
Children's Minds Margaret Donaldson, (Fontana 1978)
Teaching mathematics 3-5 Sue Gifford (Open University Press 2005)
Children and Number Martin Hughes (1986 Basil Blackwell)
Supporting mathematical development in the early years Linda Pound (2006 Open University Press)
Young Children Learning Barbara Tizard and Martin Hughes (Fontana 1984)
Children's Mathematics Maulfry Worthington and Elizabeth Carruthers (2006 Paul Chapman Publishing)

Where to find out more
Transitions and Learning Through the Life Course K. Ecclestone, G. Biesta and M. Hughes (Routledge 2009)
Change and Becoming Through the Life Course K. Ecclestone, G. Biesta and M. Hughes (Routledge 2009)

Her life

Lilian Katz was born in England but has spent the vast majority of her life in the United States of America. She is a Professor at the University of Illinois; the Director of ERIC (a comprehensive database of educational research and information); and was the founding editor of the Early Childhood Research Quarterly (claimed to be the first peer-referenced early childhood journal).

Lilian Katz is widely regarded as a leader in the field of early childhood education. At the symposium which celebrated her achievements, Petersen (2000, citing DuPree) described her as 'having integrity in all things, understanding the servanthood of leadership, and engaging in the practice of equity'. Moreover, she suggested that Katz was regarded as a strong leader because she can 'clearly articulate priorities, establish a tone or "feel" in an organization or profession, and consistently think and communicate at a level just above where the majority of people function'.

These writers are not alone in having such high regard for Lilian Katz. Throughout her long career she has written widely, spoken persuasively at untold numbers of conferences, researched, taught and communicated effectively at local, national and international levels. Her commitment springs from her respect for children and for what she herself has termed the "life of the mind" (Katz & Chard, 1989).

Her writing

For full information on what Katz has written see http://ceep.crc.uiuc.edu/pubs/katzsym/bibliography.pdf. That bibliography shows that she has been writing for five decades and in that time

Lilian Katz

has written an enormous amount. Perhaps her best known book is one entitled *Engaging Children's Minds* which she wrote with Sylvia Chard in 1989. However, Katz is probably better known for her talks than her writing and it is her inspirational public speaking for which she is most acclaimed.

Her theory

The fact that Katz has been writing and speaking, teaching and researching for such a long time means that she has put forward many ideas. The symposium which was held for her in 2000 gives a useful key to identifying the main strands of her theories. The subjects discussed there were:

- the project approach
- early years curricula
- diversity
- teacher education, and
- dispositions as goals.

In talking and writing about the project approach Katz is careful to define her terms. She is not talking about themes or topics around which adults hang the learning they have identified as their key objectives. She is describing 'a piece of in-depth research' undertaken by children. She suggests that a project is determined by children's interests and is based on their ideas, questions and experiences. Its overall aims are around establishing community ethos and providing education for democracy and it should involve learning to:

- Decide
- Argue a point
- Explain
- Predict
- Hypothesise
- Check
- Initiate
- Record
- Report
- Suggest
- Encourage and
- Accept responsibility

It can easily be seen how this focus on learning through projects fits with her other key aspects of theory. Much of her work has focused on developmentally appropriate curricula and she shows great enthusiasm for the approaches adopted in Reggio Emilia (see *How Children Learn 1* page 52). She believes strongly in the need to focus on children's learning dispositions and to challenge them intellectually. She makes a distinction between 'intellectual' and 'academic' learning. The latter she believes relates to what the setting or institution needs rather than what matters for the lifelong learning of the child.

Katz's writing and speaking are often concerned with ways of educating those who educate our youngest children. A glimpse at the ERIC website (www.eric.ed.gov), which Katz helped to establish, will give a flavour of how much she values teacher education. That website and rigorous journal articles included there have made an enormous contribution to enabling practitioners to get more information.

Diversity is a key issue in American early childhood education and has been for a very long time. You have only to think about David Weikart and the High/Scope initiative (see *How Children Learn 1* page 56) or Vivian Gussin Paley's book *White Teacher* (see page40 of this book). But it is also a particular issue in relation to quality since much of the low cost childcare provision in America is of very low quality and therefore poses a serious issue in relation to diversity. The whole of the Head Start programme, from which High/Scope emerged, was dedicated to tackling inequalities as, it is claimed, is the more recent No Child Left Behind programme in the United States.

Putting the theory into practice

Much of Katz's work was dedicated to creating teacher education programmes which tackle the issue of the gap between theory and practice. In an article about the "Katzian Early Childhood Teacher Preparation System", VanderVen describes students taking courses and practitioners undergoing in-service training who appear unable or unwilling to put what they have been taught into action. The guiding principles of a more effective approach Katz suggests include:

- Teaching practitioners in ways which reflect what they will do with children. The two would not be identical but would be consistent.
- Practitioners should have a good grasp of developmental theory so that they can check their working knowledge and understanding against theory.
- Although studying about children should be enjoyable it should not be trivialized, but should be treated seriously.
- As with children, adults' learning should be considered in terms of knowledge, skills, dispositions and feelings.

One of Lilian Katz's major abilities is translating theory into terms that are easy to communicate and easily understood by all in practice. As an example, in a booklet entitled *Five Perspectives on Quality in Early Childhood Programs*, Katz identifies as one of the five perspectives, what she calls the 'bottom-up perspective' - namely that of the child. Listed below are the questions which she suggests practitioners ask themselves on behalf of the children with whom they are working:

- Do I usually feel welcome rather than captured?
- Do I usually feel that I am someone who belongs rather than someone who is just part of the crowd?

- Do I usually feel accepted, understood, and protected by the adults, rather than scolded or neglected by them?
- Am I usually accepted by some of my peers rather than isolated or rejected by them?
- Am I usually addressed seriously and respectfully, rather than as someone who is "precious" or "cute"?
- Do I find most of the activities engaging, absorbing, and challenging, rather than just amusing, fun, entertaining, or exciting?
- Do I find most of the experiences interesting, rather than frivolous or boring?
- Do I find most of the activities meaningful, rather than mindless or trivial?
- Do I find most of my experiences satisfying, rather than frustrating or confusing?
- Am I usually glad to be here, rather than reluctant to come and eager to leave?

These are questions that are easily understood but searching and demanding reflective answers. Katz reminds the reader that "assessing the quality of bottom-up experience requires making inferences about the subjective states of the children. Ideally, these inferences would be based on extensive contact and frequent observation and information-gathering by participants over extended periods of time."

Her influence

It would be difficult to overestimate the influence of Lilian Katz. Peterson (2000) describes her as the "invisible mentor" for practitioners at all levels from professors to unqualified assistants. For her this involves "qualities of leadership, exceptional intellect, respect, extraordinary perception, and an affinity for childhood".

She suggests that this wide-ranging influence stems from her:

- **qualities of dignity** (i.e., respect for the child, admiration for the work of teaching);
- **taking the long-term view** (i.e., childhood is about the quality of life now and in the future); and
- **depth of substance** (i.e., children's minds are not for filling with cuteness, trivial fun, and inaccurate information; teaching is not a casual pursuit, and not everyone should teach).....
- **validity** (i.e., what she proposes is real, true, and germane—our sense of what is right is clarified and affirmed);
- **relevance** (i.e., the best mix of theory, practice, and reflection—our minds are not wasted when we listen); and, finally,
- **resilience** (i.e., perseverance, intuition, and humour—our minds have new connections that are forever changed)."

Comment

It is difficult to be critical of Katz's theories. She writes and speaks persuasively but she always appears to have the key issues at her fingertips and to genuinely respect children and their right to have their thinking respected. These values are consistently reflected in her work.

One possible criticism concerns the relationship between theory and practice. Everything which she writes about collaboration, dispositions and education for democracy is unarguable and yet the examples from practice which are sometimes used do not always appear to illustrate the key elements. The descriptions of practice do not always seem to match up to the high aspirations set by the theories. Is this inevitable or is it simply that the verbal descriptions cannot match up to seeing and hearing what actually goes on? Yet Paley, for example, does manage to convey to readers the rich environment in which the children are operating.

One small example may convey this gap. In their introduction to *The Project Approach*, Katz and Chard state that projects are often confined to work with small numbers of children, yet the firefighter example which features in that book talks not only about the whole class but about the relationship between the morning and afternoon groups. Another example comes from the writing of one of Katz's major supporters. Katz is reported as saying "let's call a one-year moratorium on dinosaurs" at a time when there was "an absolute craze for dinosaurs reflected on television, in toys, and in every preschool classroom in the land" (quoted by VanderVen 2000). It is difficult to square this comment with the idea that we should be building on children's interests.

Points for reflection
- Do you think there are children's interests on which we should not build?
- Reread the questions Katz asks from the child's persepctive. Are they the right questions in your view?

References
Engaging Children's minds: The Project Approach. Lilian Katz and Sylvia Chard (Ablex 1989)
Invisible Mentor: Communication Theory and Lilian Katz K. Peterson, and
New Perspectives on Theory to Practice: Implications for Transforming Teacher Education and Child Outcomes K VanderVen, (Both from Proceedings of the Lilian Katz Symposium 2000) (http://ceep.crc.uiuc.edu/pubs/katzsympro.html)

Where to find out more
www.eric.ed.gov

Ferre Laevers

In early childhood circles, Ferre Laevers is the name most commonly associated with the concepts of well-being and involvement. However, his work is widely used in this country as part of the EEL project. There is also considerable international interest in children's well-being. A recent UNICEF study of children's well-being placed Britain and the United States of America very low in international comparisons.

His life

Ferre Laevers is Director of the Research Centre for Experiential Education, based at the Department of Education, Leuven University in Belgium. He is also President of the European Early Childhood Education Research Association.

The centre for experiential education, which he established more than thirty years ago undertakes practice-orientated research, development and dissemination. Projects are conducted in collaboration with institutes, agencies and departments of education in at least 20 countries.

His writing

Much of Laevers' writing about well-being and involvement is in the form of self-evaluation documents. He disseminates his work widely, speaking and researching all over the world. Two books (both published by Leuven University) which have been translated into English are *Defining and Assessing Quality in Early Childhood Education*; and *The Involvement of Children and Teacher Style: insights from an international study in experiential education*.

His theory

Laevers' work around experiential education began in Flanders in 1976. He worked initially with a group of 12 teachers, his research driven by seeking to understand and define the notion of 'deep-level-learning'. For Laevers such learning requires a high level of involvement - which in turn is related to adult engagement - which emphasizes sensitivity, stimulation and autonomy. Laevers believes that an enabling environment, one that helps children to make connections between previous experiences, and between peers, adults and the resources available to them, is essential.

Emotional well-being is seen as being at the root of involvement - children without a sense of well-being will find it difficult to concentrate or fully engage in activities, experiences and interactions with others. His theories are related to those of humanistic psychologists such as Abraham Maslow and Carl Rogers (page 48 in this book) who suggest that feeling emotionally safe and having a good level of self-esteem make it easier to focus and learn. They also have links with the work of Csikszentmihayli (see *How Children Learn 2* page 54) and his theory of 'flow'. 'Flow' describes the deep personal satisfaction that we feel when engaged in something that challenges us, maintains our interest and rewards us in ways that are sometimes difficult to define. The term 'flow' is used by Csikszentmihayli in relation to creativity but Laevers applies it to the times when young children are lost in an experience.

Involvement

Laevers has devised the Leuven Involvement Scale to support practitioners in gauging children's level of involvement. He defines the indicators of the level of involvement as:

- Concentration
- Energy
- Complexity and creativity
- Facial expression and composure
- Persistence
- Precision
- Reaction time
- Verbal expression
- Satisfaction

The table opposite shows how involvement is graded through observation of children's activity:

Level 1	Little or no activity	This score is given to children who do not participate in activities, stare idly in front of them, are completely absent-minded or are sitting listlessly in a corner. They may seem completely uninterested or may engage in very repetitious activity. (However, children who are doing nothing may be thinking deeply or watching intently - the signs show how involved they are.)
Level 2	Moments of interrupted or sporadic activity	Children may spend less than half of their time actively engaged. THey may dream or wander about apparently aimlessly. They may focus on activities that are well below their capabilities.
Level 3	More or less sustained activity, or activity which lacks intensity	Children at this level are usually engaged in some kinds of activity, but the signs of involvement are generally absent. They are indifferent or lack energy. Their work or play does not really affect them.
Level 4	Intense activity	These children are usually active, we frequently notice signs of involvment. The activity has real meaning for them. These children often function near the boundaries of their capacity. They are not easily distracted. Yet there are moments when these children need an adult or other children to help keep them involved.
Level 5	Sustained intense activity	These children often show involvement in their activities and very easily reach a high level of involvement. These children find it easy to make choices, and once they have started an activity, they are clearly absorbed by it. They are intrinsically motivated to continue and display signs of concentration, persistence, energy and complexity.

(based on *Growing together at the Pen Green Centre*)

Well-being

Laevers' defines the key characteristics of emotional well-being as follows:

- Feeling at ease
- Acting spontaneously
- Being open to the world around
- Expressing an inner relaxation
- Showing vitality and self-confidence
- Being in touch with ones' own feelings and emotions
- Enjoying life

Wider views of well-being

A recent UNICEF study indicated that British children well-being is low when compared to children in other industrialised nations. The study looked at six indicators of well-being which were:

- Material well-being
- Family and peer relationships
- Health and safety
- Behaviour and risks
- Educational well-being
- Subjective well-being

This ties in with the concerns of several writers and thinkers who have for some time been expressing concerns about children's well-being in this country (see for example Sue Gerhardt and Sue Palmer).

Putting the theory into practice

Laevers' research began in practice and has remained firmly rooted there. As well as gauging children's level of involvement practitioners might also think about whether the activities that are sometimes imposed on children are either worthy or high levels of involvement or likely to generate it. Colouring in, worksheets and tracing are examples of activities which could (and perhaps should) be reviewed in the light of Laevers' work. Some apparently less-worthy tasks, such as playing Batman, might actually be generating much higher levels of involvement and therefore provide a better educational foundation for learning.

The ten-point action plan which Laevers has devised is also helpful in putting his theories into practice. He suggests that these will support the development of involvement in young children:

1. Rearrange the classroom in appealing corners or areas
2. Check the content of the corners and replace unattractive materials by more appealing ones
3. Introduce new and unconventional materials and activities
4. Observe children, discover their interests and find activities that meet these orientations
5. Support ongoing activities through stimulating and enriching interventions
6. Widen the possibilities for free initiative and support them with sound rules and agreements
7. Explore the relations with each of the children and between children and try to improve them, where necessary
8. Introduce activities that help children to explore the world of behaviour, feelings and values
9. Identify children with emotional problems and work out sustaining interventions
10. Identify children with developmental needs and work out interventions that engender involvement within the problem area.

(based on action points presented on www.european-agency.org/assessment/resourceguide/documents/2008/11/Laevers.pdf)

His influence

Laevers' work has had enormous influence internationally. In this country its influence has largely developed through the Effective Early Learning Project (EEL). The project's directors Chris Pascall and Tony Bertram have established an accredited training programme which makes use of the Leuven Involvement Scale. This has been a very successful programme and has been widely taken up in many parts of the country.

Without doubt one of the reasons for the influence and success of Laevers' work is the scoring system. In a political climate where measures and targets are regarded as very valuable a system for quantifying what may seem to the lay person like a child's random activity is seen as very helpful.

Comment

Paradoxically it is perhaps this very aspect of Laevers' work which can be seen as a weakness or a basis for criticism. Some people ask whether we should be attempting to quantify qualitative aspects of children's learning, play and development.

The other possible area of criticism lies in the focus within the scale on lone activity. Laevers' current work is focusing on social interaction but given how important we know social development to be to learning it is perhaps insufficiently addressed.

Refection points

■ Do you agree with Laevers' list of characteristics of well-being? What would you add or omit?

References

Effective Early Learning: case studies in improvement Chris Pascal and Tony Bertram (Paul Chapman Publishing 1997)
Growing together at the Pen Green Centre (www.pengreen.org)

Where to find out more
A Process-oriented child follow-up system for young children, Ferre Laevers (Centre for Experiential Education Leuven 1997)

Janet Moyles

Her life

Janet Moyles is Professor Emeritus at Anglia Ruskin University. She has worked there for a number of years supporting research activities. She was chair of the early childhood organisation *Training, Advancement and Co-operation in Teaching Young Children* (TACTYC) for seven years and now edits the TACTYC newsletter and website. Janet has also been an active member of the Early Years Curriculum Group for many years.

Janet was herself an early years practitioner working in a range of settings as well as a primary headteacher. This connection between early years provision and primary education is reflected in much of her work, with a laudable and frequent reiteration of the call for the early years to include key stage one.

Her writing

A prolific writer and editor, Janet has a large number of publications many of which focus on the early years. The remaining publications are about primary education. In fact her earliest books were focused on this phase of education. In 1988, she published a book entitled *Self-evaluation: a guide for primary teacher*, and in 1992 Organising for learning in the primary classroom.

Her focus on play was highlighted in 1989 with the publication of *Just Playing*. This was followed up in 1994 with the first edition of *The Excellence of Play*, which is now approaching its third edition.

Much of Janet's writing arises from her research projects. She undertook a study for the Association of Teachers and Lecturers, in conjunction with Mary-Jane Drummond (see page 20 of this book), on reception classes. This was entitled *Inside the foundation stage: recreating the reception year*. StEPs (*a Statement of entitlement to play: a framework for playful teaching*), which was published in 2001, was based on action research with teachers. Both SPEEL (2002), which focused on effective pedagogy in the early years, and *Effective Leadership and Management in the Early Years* (2006) were based on research projects.

Her research and theory

A major characteristic of Moyles' research is the active involvement of teachers and practitioners. Perhaps most notable is the development of a research process which is called 'reflective dialogue'. In The Study of Pedagogical Effectiveness in Early Learning (SPEEL), Moyles developed this technique. Practitioners were asked to identify video footage of their practice, which they themselves regarded as effective. This was then discussed with a researcher, with action points possibly being raised. These in turn could then be further discussed at subsequent sessions with new pieces of video material.

Both the ELMs project (Effective Leadership and management in the Early Years) and StEPs (Statements of entitlement to play) project illustrate Janet's commitment to the active involvement of practitioners. Rather than being viewed as subjects, they are regarded and treated as co-researchers. The ELMs project involved practitioners from Essex. Practitioners were heavily involved from the start, forming a focus group; active partners in the process of generating and refining the materials and providing examples. A detailed evaluation tool emerged from the process - highlighting leadership qualities; management skills; professional skills and attributes; as well as the personal characteristics and attitudes required of a leader in the early years.

With StEPs, a group of practitioners met together over two years, discussing, analysing, challenging and reflecting. So committed to the process were the group that members continued to meet after the funding for the project had run out. The group generated over 100

LINKS

- *How Children Learn 3*
  Drummond

Janet Moyles

Diagram 2: Moyles' play spiral

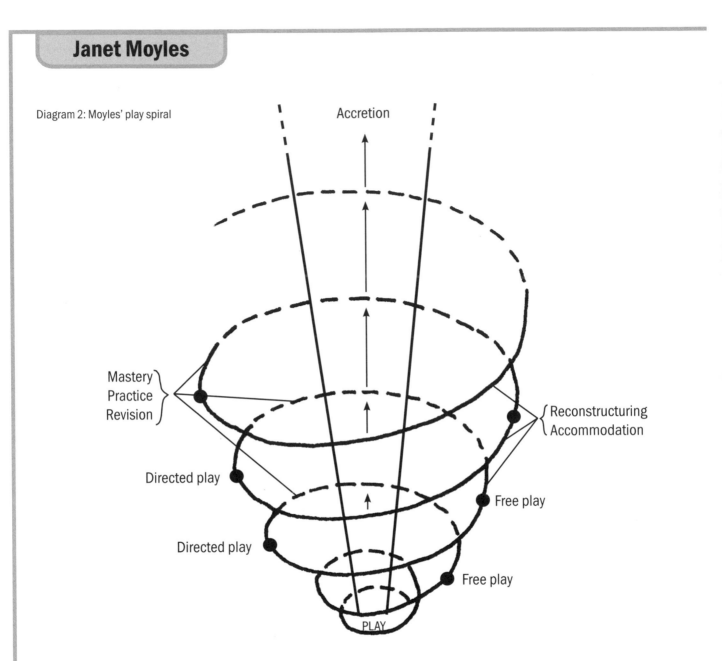

Accretion

Mastery
Practice
Revision

Reconstructuring
Accommodation

Directed play

Free play

Directed play

Free play

PLAY

principles which, through time and negotiation, were formed into six Statements of Entitlement to Play (stEPs). These were as follows:

■ Young children are entitled to play experiences that engage them affectively and socially in their own and others' learning.

■ Young children are entitled to play experiences that are set in meaningful and relevant activities and contexts for learning.

■ Young children are entitled to play experiences that promote curiosity and the use of imagination and creativity in learning.

■ Young children are entitled to engage in play experiences that are open-ended and offer trial-and-error learning without fear of failure.

■ Young children are entitled to playful, exploratory and experiential activities with a variety of contexts.

■ Young children are entitled to engage in individual and dynamic play and learning experiences relevant to their age group and stage of development.

Perhaps the aspect of research and thinking most widely associated with Janet Moyles' work is the subject of play. In *Just Playing*, she included the concept of a 'play spiral', see diagram 2 above. Spiral models are popular in education. For example, Bruner wrote about 'the spiral curriculum' and Keith Swanwick produced a spiral model to demonstrate musical development. Moyles describes her spiral:

The process is actually cyclical .... Rather like a pebble on a pond, the ripples from the exploratory free play allowed a spiral of learning spreading ever upwards into wider experiences for the children and upwards into the accretion of knowledge and skills. (Just Playing, page 15)

In later work (2005), Moyles highlights the notion of 'playful pedagogy'. She concludes by reminding the reader that politicians emphasise the importance of a 'learning society', but adds "it seems unlikely that this will be a reality unless the earlier play-learning suggests to children that learning and understanding is something exciting.....This requires practitioners committed to adult engagement and interaction in children's play, be it as models, providers, enhancers, initiators, advocates or contributors."

Putting the theory into practice

As both a practitioner and a highly practical person, Janet Moyles's work is very much focused on the relationship between theory and practice. Her approach to research is, as we have seen, rooted in practice and her writing is littered with cameos, case studies and examples drawn from practice. This makes her work accessible and therefore popular. Her earliest writing took the form of self evaluation guidance and her work on leadership echoes that. In StEPs for example each video sequence includes details of the entitlement involved, the area(s) of learning and development addressed, and an activity plan. All the statements of entitlement include an analysis to support practitioners that highlights:

- what the children featured in the sequence already know
- what aspect of development the learning involved demonstrates (e.g. playful, social etc.)
- what children still need to learn
- what professional knowledge and understanding adults need
- what provision needs to be made
- what should be taught.

In addition, many of her publications include annotated bibliographies - listing not simply helpful books but some indication of what they cover. This is an important aspect of Moyles' work - seeking not just to change practice but wanting to give practitioners the tools and knowledge they need to decide when, how and why things need changing.

Her influence

In the SPEEL report, Moyles suggests that reflection is what a practitioner teacher does when looking back or reviewing the teaching and learning that has occurred. It involves going back over what happened, what emotions were involved and what was achieved. She writes that "it is that set of processes through which a professional learns from experience... chang(ing) .. behaviour and attitude". Perhaps Moyles' greatest influence has been in encouraging the reflection necessary to improving and developing practice.

Janet Moyles is, along with Tina Bruce, widely regarded as 'the play lady'. Their views have some things in common, as well as some minor differences. What is important is that play is kept on the agenda - for both the public and policy makers. Janet's influence in this sphere has undoubtedly been great.

Comment

Some criticisms could arise from the difference between Moyles' views on play and those of thinkers such as Tina Bruce. While the former stresses the ways in which play can be used to support learning, the latter favours 'free-flow' play which is by its nature child-initiated. Both consider it important to develop play but for Moyles 'playful teaching' is part of a continuum of play provision. For Bruce it is a different activity.

Points for reflection

- What is your view of play? Do you favour Janet Moyles' view of play as a tool for teaching and learning or Tina Bruce's view of free-flow play?

References

Self-evaluation: a guide for primary teacher, Janet Moyles (Open University Press 1988)
Organising for learning in the primary classroom, Janet Moyles. (Open University Press 1992)
Just Playing, Janet Moyles (Open University Press 1989)
The Excellence of Play, Janet Moyles (Open University Press 1994/ 2nd edition 2005)
Inside the foundation stage: recreating the reception year. Janet Moyles et al (ATL 2001)
Study of pedagogical effectiveness in early learning (SPEEL) Janet Moyles et al (DfES 2002) (dcfs.gov.uk/research/data/upload files/RR363.pdf)
StEPs (a *Statement of entitlement to play: a framework for playful teaching*) Janet Moyles and Sian Adams (Open University Press 2001)
Effective Leadership and Management in the Early Years Janet Moyles (Open University Press 2006)

Where to find out more
http://www.dcsf.gov.uk/research/data/uploadfiles/RR363.pdf

Vivian Gussin Paley and the role of narrative in learning

Vivian Gussin Paley is a remarkable woman. An American, now in her eighties, she continues to observe children and reflect on the significance of what she sees and hears. Her books are written without a single reference and yet they are insightful and inspiring. A truly reflective practitioner, Paley's writing is based on recordings, transcription and analysis of the conversations of children in kindergartens.

Her life

Vivian Gussin Paley arrived in the United States of America as an immigrant from eastern Europe. She has spoken very movingly of her childhood in a video about her work. Her experiences of inequality led her to seek fairness for all.

She was a kindergarten teacher for thirty-seven years and has written a large number of books which are essentially an analysis of her work. She herself suggests that although the focus of her thinking and work has always been the imaginative play of young children, the books have enabled her to develop her own self-awareness.

She is the only kindergarten teacher to ever receive one of the MacArthur "genius" grants.

Her writing

Paley tells a story about when she was a young and inexperienced teacher, and enrolled for a masters degree. After handing in her first assignment, the tutor called her aside and suggested that she would be better to write than study formally. How true that has turned out to be!

Her first book was entitled *White Teacher* and she wrote it in order to help herself to understand her role amongst a community of black children. The following are two books which stand out amongst the many that Paley has written. *Wally's Stories* (written in 1981) is one which is highlighted simply for its fun and enthusiasm. It is clear to the reader that Paley loves the children with whom she works - not in a sloppy sentimental way but in a respectful way, wanting to understand their thinking and motives. The second is *The boy who would be a helicopter* (1990). This has been the subject of focus by theatre in education companies. MakeBelieve Arts have developed Paley's story-telling/ story-acting approach into something which they call 'the helicopter technique'. MakeBelieve Arts offer training to practitioners in working with children in the way in which Paley herself does (see www.makebelievearts.co.uk).

Her theory

Paley's theories spring from her approach to curriculum, which is based around stories and play. At the heart of her kindergarten practice are opportunities for children to tell their own stories, individually to an adult who writes the story down exactly as it is told to them. Then, in each session there are story-writing sessions when the children act out one another's stories. She writes of this process (*A Child's Work*, 2004 page 3) that "in documenting and dramatizing their language, lore, and literary strivings, my purpose is to examine their curriculum in its natural form, much as they study one another through the medium of their play."

In addition, Paley is not only interested in the stories which are told to an adult, scribed and acted out, but also in the stories that are part of their day to day play. For her the two aspects - story-telling/ story-acting and imaginative play - are complementary and she analyses them to help her to understand their thinking.

Often the relationship between play and the stories that are scribed is clear. Children use events from things they have experienced and mix them freely with stories they have heard or seen, as well as those they have created in their play. She suggests that "children love to play because they love stories" (2004). She analyses and weaves these stories together to create a compelling narrative about children's understanding. She explores the shifts between fantasy and reality which are a feature of children's stories.

Many examples can be found, but the following gives a flavour of her work. A class of five year olds have planted beans which have failed to grow. Some children discover (by tipping the pots out) that the beans have disappeared. In their conversations with Paley they offer many theories about what has happened. Maybe the wind blew them away; a squirrel took them; or something disguised as a worm dissolved them.

Dismissing Paley's questions about why a robber would want them, the most popular theory by far is that the beans have been stolen. She concludes that to deal with an unseen event is too difficult to imagine and perhaps even disturbing - so the children prefer their often magical explanations which give them power in a world where adults seem to know everything.

From the hundreds of stories and examples of play which Paley describes and analyses it is possible to draw out the theory which underpins her work. For her the education of young children must include (McNamee 2005):

■ Intellectual and academic rigour. For all the humour in her exchanges with children she never talks down to them, nor does she mistake their lack of experience for a lack of insight.

■ Pretend play, since this is an essential part both of achieving academic goals and learning to live with and understand others;

■ Inclusive classrooms which enable children to operate as part of a supportive and loving community, and

■ Support in enabling young children to become morally responsible future citizens for a democratic society.

One vital aspect of her work is thinking about larger questions such as fairness and justice and about what it means to go to school - both for teachers and children.

Putting the theory into practice

It is difficult to describe putting theory into practice in relation to Paley's work since she essentially exudes theory from her practice. Her descriptions of practice give insight into the philosophy that underpins all her dealings with children. In describing Frederick, the main character in one of her books, Paley identifies 4Fs as central elements to children's thinking.

Vivian Gussin Paley

These characterise her theory:

- Fairness
- Fantasy,
- Friendship and
- Fear of losing one's special place.

Her influence

In academic circles, Paley is widely recognised for her reflective work. She has received many awards and prizes for her writing. This is a little surprising since her work is so rooted in her observations of children and so simply written. It is not however in the least surprising when one sees the insightful qualities of her writing. However, it remains a pity that her work is not better known amongst practitioners in this country. Like the pioneers of nursery education such as Susan Isaacs and the McMillan sisters, she understands children and their learning needs.

Comment

Perhaps the greatest danger in reading Paley's work (though not a trap that she falls into) is that it is all too easy to merely think how cute the children are. Although entertaining and engaging, what Paley writes about children is not designed to amuse but to give insight into the remarkable workings of their minds and imaginations.

Some critics have criticised her failure to use Standard English when writing down the children's stories. She carefully does not correct their use of English but chooses to respect the words and stories they create. The expectation is that Standard English will be learnt from the stories they hear and in their conversations with adults.

Paley has sometimes been criticised for apparently allowing undesirable aspects of children's play to remain unchecked. In *Boys and Girls: superheroes in the doll corner*, for example, she writes about boys' boisterous behaviour. Criticisms have come from those who have not understood that in describing it she is seeking to understand it - not merely to accept that 'boys will be boys'.

In her most recent work (*A child's work: the importance of fantasy play*, 2004) Paley herself criticises those who regard play as allowing too much focus on risky topics such as gun play or terrorist attacks such as 9/11. She assertively defends the role of play as a means of thinking about difficult things, describing it as 'mankind's oldest and best-used learning tool'.

Points for reflection

- Do you agree that friendship, fairness, fantasy and the fear of losing one's special place are universal characteristics of children's play?
- Observe the many ways in which children make use of narrative in their play and conversation.

References

A child's work: the importance of fantasy play Vivian Gussin Paley (University of Chicago Press 2004)
Boys and Girls: superheroes in the doll corner Vivian Gussin Paley (University of Chicago Press 1984)
The boy who would be a helicopter Vivian Gussin Paley (Harvard University Press 1990)
'The one who gathers children' GIllian McNamee *Journal of Early Childhood Teacher Education,* Issue 3, pp. 275-296
Wally's Stories Vivian Gussin Paley (Harvard University Press 1981)
White teacher Vivian Gussin Paley

Where to find out more
www.makebelievearts.co.uk

Steven Pinker

His life

Steven Pinker's first degree was in experimental psychology, gained at McGill University in Montreal. His subsequent study and research has been mainly at Massachusetts (MIT) and Harvard University. He is currently the Harvard College Professor and the Johnstone Family Professor in the Department of Psychology and has won many prizes for his books and his research.

He describes himself as an experimental psychologist who is interested in all aspects of language and mind (http://pinker.wjh.harvard.edu). Much of his initial research was around visual cognition but he gradually developed an interest in language development (especially in children), and this topic eventually took over his research activities.

His writing

Pinker writes a wide range of academic papers. In addition he writes frequently for *The New Republic*, and *The New York Times*, and has published five books for a more general audience. One writer has described these books as being "like bombs tossed into the eternal nature-versus-nurture debate".

The Language Instinct, published in 1994, was an introduction to all aspects of language, which stresses that language is a biological adaptation - a function of our genes. This was followed in 1997 by *How the Mind Works*, which offered similar arguments for other aspects of the mind including vision, reasoning, emotions, humour, and art. In 1999 he published *Words and Rules*, which presented his research on regular and irregular verbs. In 2002 he published The Blank Slate, which explored political, moral, and emotional aspects of the concept of human nature. His latest book *The Stuff of Thought* was published in 2007.

His theory

Pinker's theories are largely categorised into two groups. Firstly, he is described as an evolutionary psychologist. He argues that humans have evolved to be language-users and creators, in much the same way as a spider evolved to spin a web. Pinker is perhaps most famous for his work on language, in which he has been instrumental in popularizing the work of Noam Chomsky. Both Pinker and Chomsky regard language as an inborn facility. This view is by no means without its critics.

For evolutionary psychologists, natural selection is part of their argument and this may result in conflict. However, they also claim that we have evolved with powers of co-operation. Much of human behaviour has evolved from attempts to solve recurrent problems. Their theories suggest that, for example, humans have inherited:

- special mental capacities for acquiring spoken language
- abilities to gauge the emotions of others, and to choose healthier mates.

The second category is known as a computational theory of the mind. In this view, thinking occurs in the brain which has many of the features of a computer and is simply an information processing system. Thinking is therefore, in this theory, a form of computation.

Putting the theory into practice

Pinker has described his sister Susan Pinker who is a psychologist and counsellor as "actually trained to do something". From this we may infer that he does not see practical applications of his work as being something that he is interested in. Academic, gifted lecturer and persuasive writer, he illustrates his work with examples drawn from popular culture and everyday incidents, but putting his theories into practice is not his motivation.

Perhaps what early childhood practitioners can learn from Pinker (and his critics) is that we should not place too firm a belief in evolutionary psychology. Education is about changing behaviour and improving learning. We cannot want to create a situation where we excuse some behaviours on the grounds that children can't help behaviours that get in the way of learning because "it's in their genes!"

His influence

Pinker has been named amongst the top one hundred intellectuals and the top one hundred most influential people in the world. His books have received both strong criticism from fellow academics but, in the mind of the man or woman in the street, his theories make common sense. Perhaps Pinker's greatest influence has been in stimulating thinking and debate across many groups in society.

Comment

The most widespread criticisms of Pinker's work comes from feminist and pacifist groups who have strongly held beliefs that whether or not some behaviours are genetic we must work towards civilizing influences.

It is however from fellow scientists that the harshest criticisms have come. Stephen Jay Gould, a highly respected and influential scientist, argues against what he terms 'biological determinism'. Gould describes Pinker's theories as 'pure guess-work in the cocktail –party mode'. An evolutionary biologist, Gould opposes evolutionary psychology insisting that while evolution shaped the brain, individual people and not their genes are the unit of natural selection. He is by no means the only critic of evolutionary psychology. So strong have been the attacks, in fact, that the efforts to oppose its teaching in colleges and universities has been termed 'the new creationism.'

In a book entitled *The Language Instinct Debate*, Geoffrey Sampson praises Pinker's *How the Mind Works* and *The Blank Slate* as well-written but completely wrong. He suggests that language is acquired through the culture. He challenges the view of language acquisition taken by Pinker (and Chomsky before him). They suggest that language learning must be a question of nature since:

- it is learnt quickly, but Sampson argues that two years is not particularly fast
- it is age dependent, but if early opportunities are missed, language may never be learnt;
- children learn to talk without formal instruction, but they are constantly learning things which no one sets out to teach them;
- grammars have many common features. However

developmental psychologists suggest that this is not because of evolution but because of the way in which our brains work.

Rather more measured but equally critical views are aired in a book entitled *Rethinking Innateness*. In it a group of well-known neuroscientists challenge evolutionary psychologists. They claim that an interactionist viewpoint - with a balance between nature and nurture influencing our behaviour - is the only correct one. Many writers taking an interactionist perspective describe the balance as a dance. Elman and his colleagues describe nature and nurture as Batman and Robin hanging "around waiting in the wings, (and then they) sweep in and solve a problem and then disappear before they can be unmasked". They cite four major criticisms:

- "the way genes work probably precludes anything like 'genes for language'" - there are just too few of them
- information processing models of thinking are too linear to fully account for human thought
- it is difficult to account for many of the ways in which humans behave in solely evolutionary terms
- humans have been described as architects of their own brains - this simply means that as our contexts constantly change, so does our behaviour. We cannot afford to be servants of our genes.

In *How the Mind Works*, Pinker denies that music has any evolutionary significance. He likens it to strawberry cheesecake allowing us to experience nothing more than mental delight. A number of authors in *Communicative Musicality* (see Colwyn Trevarthen in this book page 57) challenge this view and underline the fact that Pinker has failed to recognise that music is much more than a set of notes - it has social and emotional functions. In fact, in much the same way as spoken language has!

Points for reflection
- What practical applications do you think Pinker's work might have?
- Do you agree that music is just relaxation or do you see it as fundamental?

References
Communicative Musicality Stephen Malloch and Colwyn Trevarthen (Oxford University Press 2008)
How the Mind Works Steven Pinker (Penguin 1998)
Rethinking Innateness Jeffrey Elman et al (MIT Press 1998)
The Language Instinct Steven Pinker (penguin 1994)
The Language Instinct Debate Geoffrey Sampson (Continuum 2nd ed 2006)

Where to find out more
http://pinker.wjh.harvard.edu
www.guardian.co.uk/Archive/Article/0,4273,3926387,00.html
The Stuff of Thought Steven Pinker (Penguin 2007)

Gillian Pugh

Her life

Dame Gillian Pugh was Chief Executive of The Coram Family until her retirement in 2005. She had been working there for eight years, during which time she set up the Thomas Coram Centre for Children and Families in partnership with Camden Council. The Coram Family is England's oldest children's charity. Throughout her career, she has been a pioneer in contemporary childcare services and an important contributor to government thinking on education, social care and health services support for disadvantaged children and their families.

During her time at The Coram Family the charity:

- Increased the number of children, young people and families benefiting from Coram Family's services from 300 to over 6,000 a year
- Repositioned the organisation and brought its work into the forefront of government thinking
- Established a separate charitable trust to enable the public to have access to the charity's art collection at the Foundling Museum
- Developed the Coram Community Campus as an integrated early childhood service, which has been designated as an "early excellence centre"
- Won Charity of the Year award (children and youth category) in 2003

Before taking up her post at The Coram Family, she worked at the National Children's Bureau for 22 years. During that time she succeeded in setting up the Early Childhood Education Forum (now known as ECF).

Gillian has had many different roles during her distinguished career. As a member of the Children's Workforce Development Council (CWDC); chair of the National Children's Bureau; a visiting professor at the Institute of Education; Chair of the Advisory Committee for the Review of Primary Education; an advisor to the Select Committee for Children, Schools and Families and to the DCSF; member of the committee looking at support for vulnerable and excluded children, she has consistently contributed to public understanding of the issues surrounding children and families.

Her writing

Overall Gillian Pugh has written and edited more than thirty books. Pugh's early writing focused on children and families. In 1984 she co-wrote *The Needs of Parents. Training to Work in the Early Years*, which she later co-edited with Lesley Abbott in 1998, reflects the then emerging issue about how the early years workforce could become better qualified. These books characterise her writing throughout that period with a clear focus on burning policy issues.

In 1997, the *Times Educational Supplement* (31.1.97) described Gillian Pugh as someone who "combines intellectual ability with gritty practical concern for what happens to children and their parents. She is on a mission." These qualities are reflected in her writing, which is both scholarly and accessible. She has an excellent grasp of policy issues, an encyclopaedic knowledge of related issues and a straightforward style, which makes her writing both interesting and informative. Her best-known book *Contemporary Issues in the Early Years* is now in its fourth edition. In it a range of leaders in the field of early childhood have put forward their views on current concerns.

Since her retirement from The Coram Family, Gillian has published a history of the charity entitled *London's Forgotten Children*. This has been well-received. She comments that although today 40% of babies born in this country are born 'illegitimately' i.e. out of wedlock, when the Foundling Hospital was set up in the eighteenth century, illegitimacy carried an enormous stigma. The charity was in fact not for foundlings but for illegitimate children, brought in by their mothers. Nor was it a

Dame Gillian Pugh, as she is know known, has been described by Naomi Eisenstadt (formerly national director of Sure Start) in these words: "I can think of no one in the voluntary sector who has made as significant a contribution to the well-being of children".

hospital but the first children's home, set up long before the wave of Victorian homes for orphaned and abandoned children were created.

Her commitment to such vulnerable children is reflected in another of her books *Unlocking the Past*, which explores the impact of giving children access to the records held by Barnardo's. In these and other publications, Pugh reveals her feeling that children need to have someone for whom they are special. An attachment such as this builds children's resilience despite adverse conditions in infancy.

David Lane who reviewed *London's Forgotten Children* (www. childrenwebmag.com 2nd January 2008) suggests that "the key message from the book is that providing and developing services for children and young people does not just happen. It is the result of years of hard work by people such as Thomas Coram and his supporters, who included Handel and Hogarth. It is shaped by researchers such as John Bowlby. If it is not to become outdated, it has to be adapted to new needs and circumstances by innovators who take risks in trying out new approaches."

Her theory

Gillian Pugh's lifetime of commitment to children and families embodies her theory, but how can it best be put into words? In a chapter entitled 'The Voice of the Child', which she co-wrote with Dorothy Selleck, Pugh suggests that in order to work effectively with young children adults need:

- Sufficient knowledge of child development to have appropriate expectations of children
- The ability to listen reflectively and see things from a child's point of view
- An understanding of children's representation which enables them to "observe and interpret (children's) representations, to appreciate the significance of their play, their movements, their art and music as powerful child-like voices of communication"
- A willingness to extend children's thinking and give them opportunities to communicate their ideas, thoughts and feelings
- Respect, acceptance and patience
- An ability to help children to express and manage their feelings - not negating their fear, anger, resistance and protest. The authors quote the words of Korczak, from Lifton's biography of him, The King of Children. He said that "the child has the right to protest at injustice".

Gillian Pugh's theories revolve around making things better for children and families. In her introduction to the current edition of Contemporary Issues in the Early Years she analyses the government's strategy for childcare. The issues she raises are around quality and the interface between schools and early years

provisions. She concludes in words which perhaps summarise her thinking:

As the ten-year childcare strategy rolls out, it will be important to ensure that quality of service is maintained as the quantity increases, that children's needs remain paramount, and that parents really do feel that they have choice.

Putting the theory into practice

Gillian Pugh has been credited with creating the vision of children's centres. In the 1990s, she gave a lecture in Greenwich, sponsored by the TES, in which she put forward the ideal of a school linked to an early years centre and a health centre. This was to become the starting point for the Millennium School established in the London Borough of Greenwich which was built with government funding to mark the beginning of the twenty first century.

Her theories have always been rooted in practice. Her publications have always had a practical slant - theory translating into both policy and practice. Difficult issues are not merely set out - they are explored and analysed to see whether solutions can be found. This can be clearly seen in her work setting up the Early Childhood Education Forum (now known as ECF).

Her influence

In 1997 the *Times Education Supplement* carried this report: Universally admired for her formidable networking skills, Dr Pugh has used her position as director of the NCB's early childhood unit to hone her knowledge of her subject. She has used her administrative competence as a base for making things happen on the ground locally and with ministers and civil servants nationally. As chair of the Early Childhood Education Forum, a disparate grouping of the warring tribes within early years education, she has done what no-one else could: get the tribes to pow wow.

It is surprising to the uninitiated to find such trouble in the early years field. One might expect the practitioners to sink whatever differences they have in the interests of the children in their care, but that has not always been the case. Those who look after the under-fives in nurseries run by the health or social services have been suspicious sometimes of those who care for under-fives in the education service and vice versa. Maintained nurseries have resented private ones; the voluntary sector has sometimes felt shunned by the state; and so on. Dr Pugh got them round a table.

She was determined to set up a unified organisation because she believed that without a single voice, early childhood professionals would not be listened to. She used the experience of practitioners in New Zealand to drive forward an agenda which could be heard by policy-makers.

But, her influence is not confined to the sector itself. She has also been immensely successful in creating links with politicians at all levels. It would be difficult to overestimate the influence she has had and the impact of her work in practical decisions making.

This very pragmatism - a willingness to compromise and look for solutions has not endeared Pugh to everyone. The very fact that she has determined to work with politicians and practitioners whatever their views has sometimes led those with more entrenched views on all sides to reject her views.

The *Times Educational Supplement* adds (3/1/97): "her willingness to work the system does not endear her to radicals impatient for change - or to a few venerable male educationists who find her strength of mind and character hard to take." Some of her pragmatism, however, may have sprung from the fact that she was working for NCB - an organisation which received government funding. Later, in 2006, now retired, she wrote:

The current emphasis on preparing children for school is (not) appropriate. A far more important question in my view is to ask whether schools are ready for children. We need to pay more attention to how children learn, and the role of schools overall in promoting learning, if early education is to be effective.

Points for reflection

- Do you agree that the emphasis on preparing children for school is inappropriate?
- What would make schools ready for children?

References

London's Forgotten Children: Thomas Coram and the Foundling Hospital Gillian Pugh (Tempus Publishing 2007)
The King of Children, Betty Jean Lifton (Pan Books 1988)
'Listening to and Communicating with young children', Gillian Pugh and Dorothy Selleck *In The Voice of the Child* edited by Davie et al (Routledge 1995)
Contemporary Issues in the Early Years: working collaboratively for children Gillian Pugh and Bernadette Duffy (editors) (Sage 2006)
The Needs of Parents, Gillian Pugh and Erica De'Ath (NCB 1984)
Training to Work in the Early Years Lesley Abbott and Gillian Pugh (eds) (Open University Press 1998)

Where to find out more

Contemporary Issues in the Early Years: working collaboratively for children Gillian Pugh and Bernadette Duffy (editors) (Sage 2006)
www.ncb.org.uk/ecf
www.coram.org.uk

Carl Rogers

His life

Carl Rogers was born in 1902, the fourth of six children. He was regarded as something of a prodigy, able to read well before he started kindergarten. Rogers, together with notable psychologists such as Charlotte Buhler and Abraham Maslow, developed in the 1940s what came to be known as the third force. (For more information see *How Children Learn 2* page 63). This was because it identified and rejected the limitations of both behaviourism (see *How Children Learn 1* page 42) and psychoanalytical approaches (see *How Children Learn 1* page 17). Rogers was honoured in 1956 by the American Psychological Association for his pioneering research in establishing person-centred approaches. The person-focussed approach was initially applied to therapy, but later extended to education.

His first career choice was agriculture, quickly followed by studies in history and religion. Eventually he enrolled at Teachers College, Columbia University, obtaining an MA in 1928 and a PhD in 1931. His major interest was children's studies and he went on to direct the Society for the Prevention of Cruelty to Children in Rochester, New York. Over a period of years he became increasingly interested in counselling and the way in which clients can be supported to restructure or rebuild their lives. In 1956, Rogers became the first President of the American Academy of Psychotherapists.

His writing

Rogers' first book was entitled *The Clinical Treatment of the Problem Child* and was published in 1939, based on his experience in working with troubled children. In 1942 he wrote his second book, *Counselling and Psychotherapy* while he was working as a professor of clinical psychology at Ohio State University. Probably his best-known book is entitled *On Becoming a Person*. It was written while he was teaching psychology at the University of Wisconsin and published in 1961. Altogether Rogers wrote 16 books and a large number of journal articles so his theories have been extensively described.

His theories

Rogers' work is often described as humanistic. Unlike behaviourism, humanism recognises the will of the person and the fact that humans have motives and feelings and that these cannot be ignored in human interactions. He differs from Freud in two key ways. Firstly, Freud attempted to interpret his clients' views for them. Rogers on the other hand recognised that all knowledge is subjective and that context and people alter our perception of what is happening. Secondly, Freud frequently described his clients as hysterics and has for that reason been severely criticised by feminist theorists. Rogers insists on what her termed "unconditional positive regard," which requires that we accept a person without any negative judgement.

Abraham Maslow, one of Rogers' co-founders of humanistic psychology, writes extensively about 'self-actualisation'. Rogers prefers the term 'the fully-functioning person'. Both refer to mental health and well-being. For Rogers the fully-functioning person demonstrates the following qualities:

- **Openness to experience**, including your own feelings
- **Living in the present** - rather than the future or the past
- **Trusting ourselves**, doing what feels right
- **Acknowledging freedom of choice** and taking responsibility for our decisions
- **Creativity** - for Rogers this involves helping others to become fully-functioning. This may occur through arts and sciences but may simply be through our dealings with others.
- **Reliability and constructiveness**
- **A rich full life** – he describes the life of the fully functioning individual as rich, full and exciting and suggests that they experience joy and pain, love and heartbreak, fear and courage more intensely.

Putting the theory into practice

As I began to trust students.....I changed from being a teacher and evaluator, to being a facilitator of learning.
Carl Rogers Freedom to learn for the 80s 1983

Carl Rogers is best known for his contributions to therapy, which he initially described as non-directive. As he worked he realised that this was inappropriate since clients came looking for guidance. So he changed the name to client-centred, but other therapists objected since it implied that they were not client-centred. The term most commonly used now is Rogerian therapy. One of the

phrases that Rogers used to describe his therapy is "supportive, not reconstructive," and he uses the analogy of learning to ride a bicycle to explain. Simply telling someone what to do will not work - learning must involve getting things wrong.

Reflection is key to Rogerian therapy by which Rogers meant the mirroring of emotional communication: He suggested that reflection must come from the heart, and that in order to be effective, a therapist must have three qualities which were "necessary and sufficient", since if these are present clients will improve. The qualities are:

1. **Congruence** -- genuineness, honesty with the client.
2. **Empathy** -- the ability to feel what the client feels.
3. **Respect** -- acceptance, unconditional positive regard towards the client.

Other applications of Rogers' work include education, nursing, cross-cultural relations and other caring professions. The application to education has a large robust research tradition similar to that of therapy. Rogers described the approach to education in *Client-Centered Therapy* and wrote *Freedom to Learn* devoted exclusively to the subject in 1969. *Freedom to Learn* was revised twice. The notion of learner centred education is at the root of personalised tuition and individualised programmes.

His influence

Rogers' last years were devoted to applying his theories in areas of national social conflict, and he travelled widely to accomplish this. In Northern Ireland, he brought together Protestants and Catholics; in South Africa, blacks and whites, in the United States, consumers and providers in the health field. Towards the end of his life, he was nominated for the Nobel Peace Prize for his work in South Africa and Northern Ireland.

In 2002, a study of psychologists found Rogers to be only second in his influence as a clinical psychologist to Freud and overall the sixth most influential psychologist. His last working trip was to Russia where his work was widely known and respected.

It has been suggested that Rogers' success is due to his skills as a communicator. The qualities of respect which he both advocated and exemplified in his work are still widely acknowledged beyond his chosen field. Within therapy he resisted exploring the unconscious, feeling that this left clients open to manipulation. The phenomenal growth and influence of his theories owes much to the way in which it appealed to other groups of professionals. Because of his experience with disturbed children, youth workers and others similarly involved in what is termed 'informal education' saw the application of his work to what they were attempting to achieve. It is easy to see how this also appealed to those working with young

Carl Rogers

children. The idea of child-centred or learner-centred education has much appeal for this sector. The language he used was easy to understand and his ideas were easy to relate to other sectors. The publication of *Freedom to Learn* in 1969 increased his influence in these informal education settings - chiming as it did with Piagetian child-centred approaches widely used at that time. The term 'facilitator of learning' derives directly from Rogerian therapy and continues to have great influence in education.

Comment

Critics of Rogers' work and theories suggest that their interpretation has over-emphasised individualism and placed insufficient emphasis on the importance of collaboration and learning from others. Others blame learner-centred approaches for taking too lenient a view of education and for bolstering confidence and self-esteem at the expense of hard work and perseverance.

Some critics suggest that muddling educational and therapeutic approaches is unhelpful. Educators are not therapists and should not, they suggest, attempt to meddle in these areas. On the other hand, how can education not be about supporting learners and developing in ways that will offer them fulfilling lives?

A further criticism lies in the qualities demanded of therapists by Rogers. The honesty, empathy and respect that he requires applies equally to educators. There are similarities between the role of a therapist as identified by Rogers and an educator. Moreover, many educational theorists have demanded equally unattainable qualities of those who work with our most vulnerable groups. Sonia Nieto (1999) for example writes:

> *The climate for learning..... cannot be separated from a climate in which care, concern, and love are central.....Love is at the core of good teaching because it is predicated on high standards, rigorous demands, and respect for students, their identities and their families.*

She goes on to say that without love learning cannot occur and that although some are harder than others to love, all must be included if learning is to be effective. This is very much in the spirit of Rogerian therapy.

Points for reflection
- Do you agree that love is at the core of good teaching?
- What do you understand by learner-centred education?

References
Freedom to Learn, Carl Rogers (Merrill 1969)

Where to find out more
Fifty Modern Thinkers on Education: from Piaget to the present, Joy Palmer (ed) (Routledge 2001)
http://www.nrogers.com/carlrogersbio.html

Barbara Rogoff

Her life

Barbara Rogoff is currently Professor of Psychology at the University College of Santa Cruz Foundation and holds the University of California Presidential Chair. She is a Fellow of the American Psychological Society, the American Anthropological Association, and the American Psychological Association. Her books have won a number of awards. She was, for a time, editor of the journal Human Development.

Her writing

Barbara Rogoff's best known book is *Apprenticeship in Thinking: cognitive development in social context*. It was in this book (published in 1990) that she introduced the term 'guided participation'. In 2001 an edited book entitled *Learning Together: children and adults in a school community* was published. *The Cultural Nature of Human Development*, which builds significantly on the notion of guided participation, was published in 2003.

Her theory

Key aspects of her theory include:

Guided participation - this concept builds on Vygotsky's Zone of Proximal Development (ZPD) and is fundamental to the thinking of all sociocultural theorists. It involves the mutual bridging of meanings between people in interactions. As ideas are communicated understanding on both sides is enhanced. It also involves the mutual structuring of participation. Children and caregivers and other companions together structure the situations in which children are involved. The structuring occurs through the choice of which activities children observe and engage in and through shared situations such as conversations, recounting, elaborating and listening to narratives, and in practice and play with routines and roles. Learning occurs as children participate in activities with their communities. Some of this learning will be instructional and at other times learning will be incidental to everyday life (based on Robson 2006 page 41). Cognitive development consists of individuals changing their ways of understanding, perceiving, noticing, thinking, remembering, classifying, reflecting, problem setting and solving, planning and so on - in shared endeavors with other people building on the cultural practices and traditions of communities. (Rogoff 2003 page 237)

Nature or nurture? - Rogoff advocates exploring human development by considering biological and cultural heritage in concert. She suggests that human biological development works together with cultural practices. This again has many similarities with the work of Vygotsky. Vygotsky suggested four levels or types of learning and development which involved both nature and nurture:

- the microgenetic which involves moment-to-moment learning;
- the ontogenetic which occurs over the course of a lifetime;
- the phylogenetic which involves slow developments through genetic changes; and
- cultural-historical development in which changes occur over centuries as new tools for thinking emerge.

She gives the practice of breastfeeding as an example of the way in which nature and nurture work together - the practice is natural but there are vast cultural differences in the ways in which it is used. She also uses childbirth as an example of the way in which technology influences nature - showing that the passing on of genes of individuals with large heads is being brought about through the use of caesarean sections. Rogoff further shows that our innate and genetic inheritance equips us to learn from the social contexts in which we find ourselves. She highlights

Barbara Rogoff

the use of language and other cultural tools for thinking as vital aspects of the social context.

Cultural tools for thinking - Rogoff identifies language as the key tool for thinking. She highlights the fact that babble is universal but that the development of the home language relies on babies' predisposition to notice variations in language - a cultural aspect of development. This social enculturation begins before birth as babies become familiar with the sound of the mother's voice and with the intonations of the language she speaks.

Literacy (a cultural development of oral language) is a different tool since it facilitates particular forms of thinking in different communities. (For further discussion of this see *The Cultural Nature of Human Development* page 258). Mathematics is a further tool for thinking identified by Rogoff. She highlights the role of the abacus; representing numbers on fingers (or other body parts or counters); formal calculation as taught in schools; or the metric system in developing different ways of thinking about mathematics in different cultures.

In addition, Rogoff identifies a range of other tools which support other conceptual systems. These include:

- classifications of plants or animals which support scientific thinking
- maps, diagrams and charts that support navigational systems
- stories and schematic maps that aboriginal groups in Australia use to map   routes and history
- folk psychology which support the organisation of our understanding of others. These vary from culture to culture.

Communities of learners - People of different cultures may think and solve problems differently. In developed cultures the cultural aspects of learning are highly reliant on schooling. Rogoff points out that most education systems work on a set of assumptions:

- Schooling is compulsory
- It involves segregating children from the adults within their community
- Large groups of children are isolated with (in many cases) a single adult
- Children are grouped according to their date of birth, and subjected to a standard mode of instruction which is delivered in a step-by-step form
- The skills that are taught are isolated from any productive activities
- Attempts are made to motivate children by grading their performance.

She goes on to suggest that this does not lead to effective education and that education should be more firmly rooted in cultural systems.

Putting the theory into practice

On her own website Rogoff suggests (http://psych.ucsc.edu/directory/details.php?id=21) that she is interested in the cultural aspects of:

- **Collaboration**, - by this Rogoff suggests that children should be supported in working collaboratively but collaboration must also be between parents, communities and practitioners. She goes on to suggest that in effective schools 'learning activities are planned by children as well as adults, and where parents and teachers not only foster children's learning but also learn from their own involvement with children' (Learning Together: children and adults in a school community 2001: 3).

- **Learning through observation**, in common with many educationalists and psychologists, Rogoff highlights the role of observation in understanding children and thus matching our guided participation to children's learning needs.

- **Children's interest and keen attention to ongoing events**, - practitioners must prioritize 'instruction that builds on children's interests in a collaborative way'.

- **Roles of adults as guides or as instructors** - this refers to Rogoff's work on guided participation.

- **Children's opportunities to participate in cultural activities as well as in age-specific child-focused settings** - the practice of isolating children within schools or settings deprives children of linking learning to everyday practices. For example, from work by Rogoff and Nunes (see Robson 2006) it is clear that young street vendors were perfectly able to calculate costs and change in their practical context but were unable to use their knowledge in formal school situations. In learning to play an instrument for example, it appears that children learn better when they have access to a continuum of expertise, rather than just experienced and highly skilled players. Hearing and seeing slightly older children play their instruments with less expertise helps to create a sense of a community of learners.

Her influence

Barbara Rogoff is not well-known amongst practitioners but her areas of interest are of importance to practitioners. One reason for her limited influence, despite the wide-ranging relevance and interest of her theories may be that her writing is less accessible and therefore less communicative than it could be.

Comment

One area of criticism lies in Rogoff's choice of tools for thinking. She is critical of the narrow practices of schooling but in identifying cultural tools for thinking she focuses on literacy and mathematics. This is in contrast with Kieran Egan who identifies story, poetry, music and dance as tools for thinking for young children - as they are in cultures which have no written language.

Rogoff might also be criticised for not making her writing more accessible. Her important messages deserve a wider audience.

Points for reflection

- What do you understand by the term 'guided participation'?
- What are the differences (if any) between this and ZPD?

References

Apprenticeship in Thinking: cognitive development in social context, Barbara Rogoff (Oxford University Press 1990)
Learning Together: children and adults in a school community Barbara Rogoff (Oxford University Press2002)
The Cultural Nature of Human Development Barbara Rogoff (Oxford University Press 2003)

Where to find out more
Developing Thinking and Understanding in Young Children, Sue Robson (Routledge2006)

Kathy Sylva

Her life

An American, Sylva worked with another famous American at Oxford University, Jerome Bruner. Under his direction she worked on a study which came to be known as the Oxford Pre-School Research. At that time relatively few large-scale early years research projects had been developed in this country. Since then she has been engaged in a number of highly influential and prestigious research programmes. Sylva's early work for her PhD at Harvard University had focused on play. She has commented on what she learnt from this experience, in which she took 180 toddlers out of their playgroup one by one into a play laboratory, in order to test their ability to solve problems. In discussion with Guardian reporter Karen Gold she states that "the irony of dragging children away from a natural learning experience to give them an unnatural learning experience made me realise that I wanted to study children in real settings from then on" - and she has.

The Oxford Pre-school Research Project was a three year study undertaken between 1975 and 1978. Its focus was care for the under-fives - in nursery schools, playgroups, day-care centres and at childminders. Bruner's focus, as director of the project, was "what is good care?" He himself admitted that the questions raised by his research went far beyond the scope of social scientists and that the team had "been forced to raise questions about fundamental values for which we have no answers" (Bruner 1980). He went on to suggest that he believed that "the questions will themselves be of value". This has proved to be a rather perceptive view.

Her writing

A book entitled *Childwatching at playgroup and nursery school* was written by Kathy Sylva as part of the Oxford Pre-school research in the 1980s. The book focused on what young children were actually doing. It is described on The Children's Society website as 'questioning an unbridled free play ideology'. Sylva and her colleagues devised a system of tracking a target child and recording their actions and interactions through the use of a code. This process has been used in a number of subsequent research studies and made it possible to gather and analyse a large amount of research data.

Kathy Sylva has described herself as "an ace evaluator". She describes her pleasure at identifying the patterns that emerge from complex and large scale research data - patterns which make it possible to identify statistically significant trends and indicators. She has been involved in the evaluation of the Peers Early Education Partnership (PEEP) project; the High/Scope programme when it was first introduced into this country; and the Reading Recovery programme.

Currently Sylva is probably best known for her work, alongside Edward Melhuish; Pam Sammons and Iram Siraj-Blatchford, on the EPPE project. This studied 3,000 children as they moved from pre-school into Key Stage 1. The project lasted from 1997 - 2003. Its aim was to identify the most effective forms of pre-school provision. Since that time the same children have been studied as they moved into Key Stage 2. This project is known as the Effective pre-school and Primary Education Project (EPPE3-11). Sylva says of this work "we've shown that if a child goes to a really good pre-school, it's a protection against a not very good primary school." The project is currently moving into two further phases, namely EPPSE 3-14 and EEPSE 16+ which are looking at the outcomes for students in secondary education.

Her theories and research

The key findings of the EPPE project published in 2003 identified outcomes which are directly related to day-to-day work with young children and their families. These include findings that:

- **Pre-school experience enhances children's development**. Disadvantaged children gain most, especially if the setting they attend has a good social mix of

practitioners in influencing and guiding parents vital to children's long-term success. The project developed a rating scale for the Home Learning Environment. The children of families who scored highly, regardless of income and qualifications, had higher achievements and better social and behavioural outcomes. The index includes:

- Reading to a child
- Teaching songs and rhymes
- Painting and drawing
- Taking children on visits
- Offering opportunities for children to play with friends at home.

- **Children who play are more effective problem-solvers**. They are able to come up with more new ideas and are more relaxed. They have fewer frustrations and less fear of failure. "We get more and more confident that there really is something about play-based and informal education for children before school that really is beneficial. It's more important that they play than have a formal education."

Putting the theory into practice

Just as a dripping tap takes time to fill a bucket so the attitudes of the general public, politicians and policy makers cannot be changed overnight. They have however been changed - and continue to do so - in the thirty years since Kathy Sylva came to work in this country. Sylva's theories are often put into practice at a policy level.

The Oxford Pre-school research project underlined the lack of clear strategic direction for services for young children and commented on the fragmentation both of provision itself and of responsibility for such provision. Its findings were highly controversial at the time since they indicated, for example, that there was insufficient difference between provision in playgroups and in nursery schools to justify the immense difference in cost. It went on to underline the disadvantaging effects of the fact that there were at that time insufficient nursery places for all three and four your olds whose parents wanted it.

Similarly Sylva's High/Scope work has also influenced practice and policy. The long-term impact of High/Scope which Sylva did much to highlight in this country (see for example her chapter in Early Education Transformed) was to lead to the setting up of Sure Start.

Some of the findings of the EPPE project, such as the need for sustained shared conversation, requires a re-assessment of the way in which staff work with children and can have a direct effect on practice. On the other hand, while you may have no direct control over policy decisions such as children's attendance patterns, it is important to understand and to be prepared to talk about the impact on children of policy decisions. Early years practitioners are experts

children. "For a poor child, not going to pre-school (is) like tying their hands behind their backs for the rest of primary school."

- **Longer periods of attendance overall improve independence, concentration and the ability to get along with others**. Intellectual development is also improved. However full-time provision does not of itself offer advantages over part-time provision.

- **Good quality provision may be found in all kinds of setting**. However it was most consistently high in integrated centres, nursery schools and nursery classes. Settings where staff and particularly managers had higher qualifications offered better outcomes for children. Where appropriately qualified teachers are involved provision is also enhanced.

- **Opportunities for sustained, shared conversation and thinking with children promote effective learning**.
- **Parents and carers make a real impact on children's learning**. What parents do with children at home makes a difference, and this makes the work of

Kathy Sylva

working in early childhood care and education, has been highly influential amongst policy makers and practitioners. She has brought hard-edged quantitative research methods to a field of provision that has been traditionally viewed as not open to such methods.

Sylva's long-term involvement with government has the potential to place her in a difficult position. Recommendations arising from her research about the involvement of qualified teachers in early years settings have not been as readily accepted by politicians as she would have wished. Sylva suggests that this is because it would be expensive to implement. Although the EPPE projects are all government funded she has generally managed to steer a steady course. She supports the government's record on early years but has not been afraid to challenge on issues. For example, she has challenged some of the early learning goals as overly ambitious for young children. This has been achieved against a background of research objectives which were initially distrusted by many practitioners. However, over time the research process has underlined the importance of play, conversation and social and emotional well-being. Sylva has been and remains highly influential in getting this message across to politicians - she has a voice that is heard and respected.

Points for reflection
- Why do you think that children who play might be more effective problem-solvers?
- How can (or should) practitioners help parents to improve their ratings on the Home Learning Environment scales?

References
Play: its role in development and evolution Jerome Bruner,
A. Jolly and Kathy Sylva, (Pelican Books 1985)
Under Fives in Britain Jerome Bruner (Grant McIntyre 1980)
Childwatching at Playgroup and Nursery School Kathy Sylva
(Grant McIntyre 1980)
Assessing quality in the early years Kathy Sylva et al (Trentham Books 2003)
The effective provision of pre-school education (EPPE) project: findings from the pre-school period Kathy Sylva et al (2003)
Research brief: RBX15-03 (downloadable from websites shown below)
'The Role of Research in explaining the past and shaping the future' Kathy Sylva in *Early Education Transformed* Lesley Abbott and Helen Moylett (eds) (Falmer Press 1999)

Where to find out more
http://eppe.ioe.ac.uk/eppe
www.ioe.ac.uk/projects/eppe
www.dcsf.gov.uk/research

in their field and need to feel not only entitled but obliged to let other people know what you know.

Her influence

Sylva's influence cannot be denied. She has developed research findings which underpin theories and which in turn are being put into practice. Along the way she has developed useful research techniques and found ways to make her research findings accessible to politicians and practitioners. Perhaps her most positive influence has been in enabling politicians and policy makers to understand the issues that face early years education.

Comment

Sylva's work has often attracted criticism. The publication of the Oxford Pre-school research was critical of existing practice in early childhood care and education. Her work around High/Scope was regarded by many as demonstrating her failure to understand the nature of what has been termed as 'traditional early childhood curricula' in this country. The EPPE report, although controversial amongst those

Colwyn Trevarthen

His life

Colwyn Trevarthen is Emeritus Professor of Child Psychology and Psychobiology at the University of Edinburgh. He also holds an Honorary Doctorate in Psychology from the University of Crete, and he has been elected Fellow of the Royal Society of Edinburgh and Member of the Norwegian Academy of Sciences and Letters. He is on the advisory board of the Pen Green Research Centre and is vice-president of the British Association for Early Childhood Education.

Trevarthen was born and educated in New Zealand but has spent most of his academic life in Edinburgh having joined the department in 1971. After doctoral and post-doctoral research on perceptuo-motor and cognitive functions of the cerebral hemispheres, he worked with Jerome Bruner at Harvard in 1966. His work there has been described as 'pathfinding investigations on the infant mind'. Using film and video footage Trevarthen was amongst the first to show that babies as young as two months were more skilled and expressive in face-to-face communication than had previously been believed.

His writing

Colwyn Trevarthen continues to be an active researcher, thinker and theorist. He is a much sought-after speaker since he puts forward his theories in a way that underlines his continued enthusiasm and respect for children's thinking and with humour. Moreover, his talks are usually illustrated with video footage of babies - an attractive combination of communicative approaches.

Trevarthen writes a great many chapters for other people's books and research papers, but for someone with so much to say of such great importance, Trevarthen has written few books. In 1990 he edited a book on the brain, and another in 1998 on autism. *Communicative Musicality*, published in 2008, was edited jointly by Trevarthen and Stephen Malloch, a musician and acoustic expert. It explores the intrinsic musical nature of human interaction. The theory of communicative musicality has been developed from Trevarthen's groundbreaking studies showing how in mother/infant communication there exist elements of musicality - involving patterns of timing and pulse, variations in the way in which the voice is used, and gesture or movement. Without intending to, the exchange between a mother and her infant follow many of the rules of musical performance, including rhythm and timing. This is the first book to be devoted to this topic.

His research and theory

For the past 30 years, Trevarthen's research with infants and toddlers has focused on communication, including the role of emotions in development from birth. Daniel Stern, a well-known and respected developmental psychologist has suggested that Trevarthen first identified and named the concept of

Colwyn Trevarthen

intersubjectivity in 1977. However, Trevarthen generously refers to a number of other theorists (2008) from whom he claims to have learnt about the communicative abilities of babies. Whichever it is, Trevarthen has undoubtedly increased understanding of the communicative abilities of even very young babies.

Intersubjectivity refers to the interactions between adults and babies which Trevarthen suggests is innate or intuitive. Dan Siegel, Daniel Stern and others interested in the development of human minds and communication share the view that newborn infants are born with a facility for puzzling out the differences between theirs and others brains. They learn to share these with others - generally their mothers.

Protoconversation, a term particularly associated with Trevarthen and Bruner, refers to the two-way interactions that go on between adults, especially mothers, and babies. In *Communicative Musicality*, Trevarthen describes some protoconversations:

> *Examples of extremely close coordination of the infant's rudimentary vocalizations of pleasure or excitement with the baby talk of the mother are everywhere to be seen. Apparently, both partners are participating in a single rhythmical beat, as in music. Such timing of the acts of the infant to engage in the same rhythm as that of the mother's actions has been encountered in the majority of the detailed analyses we have made of fully developed communication. Thus the infant and mother generate a pattern of intention together. Usually, their acts alternate or complement one another."*

Empathy neurons is Trevarthen's term for mirror neurons (see the section entitled Brain and Body in this book). He suggests that, in imitating others, babies are not simply learning but engaging in an emotionally-charged act of communication.

Trevarthen is also interested in how the rhythms and emotions of children's play and fantasy, musical games and songs, stories and acts of discovery, with real or imaginary companions, support cultural learning in infancy and preschool years. This in turn has led to the development of his interest in music and what he has termed a theory of 'communicative musicality'. His current work investigates the rhythms and expressions of 'musicality' in vocal and gestural movement, which he believes are the foundation for communicating with children, and supporting their learning and development.

Putting the theory into practice

Trevarthen's research interests are not purely academic. He is also interested in how parents, teachers and clinicians can support children's development. His interest in the way in which musicality underpins communication and his observations on infant emotions has led to an interest in nonverbal therapies including music therapy.

Besides writing on this subject, he has been involved in founding a centre for music therapy in Bosnia Herzegovina.

Trevarthen is also interested in the role of culture in learning. He has suggested that "a child is born 'cultural', that is, born with a disposition for engagement in intense emotional interaction with other human beings, which then immediately activates a process of enculturation". His theories point out the way in which this is to be seen in practice - discussing for example the way in which young mothers use pop songs rather than traditional rhymes to interact with their babies. They do however adapt the songs to fit in with the universal rules of 'motherese', the special use of language and music which adults use with babies.

Observation is the main key to Trevarthen's understanding and he also believes it to be the key to practitioners' understanding. Building on work concerning parent-baby interactions and 'motherese', he has revealed similar rhythms and tone in teachers' expression, which he calls 'teacherese'. He has demonstrated the importance of this form of interaction to collaborative learning and to children's confidence in expressing their understanding.

His interest in babies has meant his close involvement in guidance for Scottish practitioners working with babies and toddlers up to the age of three. He has collaborated with Helen Marwick to produce for the Scottish Executive a review of all the relevant research findings in order to support the growth of evidence-based practice.

His influence

Many of the students with whom he has been involved at Edinburgh University have gone on to be highly influential themselves. Lynne Murray, for example, has produced important work on the impact of mothers' depression on children's social and language development. His interest in musicality chimes with the work of a number of theorists and researchers from many different fields or disciplines. Evolutionary psychologists, anthropologists, musicians and archeologists are all working to understand the role of music in human development. Trevarthen has long been at the forefront of this interest, but his recent writing on communicative musicality, developed with Stephen Malloch during his supposed retirement, has been welcomed by both musicians and psychologists.

Colwyn Trevarthen has also been instrumental in helping practitioners and others to respect the power of the human mind and to understand that this power is already evident in the actions of a baby. He writes of the way in which:

> *Innate, intuitive powers of the mind in a brain that moves the thousands of muscles in the body with such sensitive awareness of what will happen, are not properly understood by a psychology that accepts a model of consciousness, intelligence and*

personality, that focuses only on the cognitive processing of information.

He continues:

a richer, more common sense philosophy is gaining ground. ...Every live human person has some of this intuitive capacity to share intentions and feelings, and to make friends.
                    (Communicative Musicality 2008)

Comment

Although there are few criticisms of Trevarthen's theories, postmodern deconstructive theories have been highly critical of such developmental theories. Burman in particular criticises the notion of a predisposition to being social. She singles out intersubjectivity as being too reliant on what she terms "an impoverished and insufficiently analysed understanding of what it means to be social". She suggests that not all the studies - she singles out the studies of Bradley, who was Trevarthen's student - have been successfully replicated. That is to say that other researchers have not been able to come up with similar results. She goes on to suggest that even where results are verified their meaning has been over generalised, taking insufficient account of cultural differences. Even if these criticisms were justified in 1994, fifteen years later they can not easily be upheld.

A second area for comment is about music. See the section on Pinker for more detail.

Points for reflection
- Do you think babies are born social - or do adults simply interpret their actions as though they were interacting?

References
Communicative Musicality edited by Stephen Malloch and Colwyn Trevarthen (Oxford University Press 2008)
How the mind works Steven Pinker (Penguin Books 1997)
'Intuition for Human Communication' by Colwyn Trevarthen In *Promoting Social Interaction for Individuals with Communication Impairments* edited by Suzanne Zeedyk (Jessica Kingsley Publishers 2008)
Review of *Childcare and the Development of Children aged 0-3: Research Evidence and Implications for Out-of-Home Provision* Colwyn Trevarthen and Helen Marwick (Scottish Executive 2002)
Deconstructing Developmental Psychology Erica Burman (Routledge 1994)

Where to find out more
www.literacytrust.org.uk

Gordon Wells

PROFILE

Gordon Wells is probably best known for his work as the director of the Bristol Language Development study. However, since that time he has undertaken a great deal of thinking and research about the role of dialogue in learning and teaching.

KEY DATES

1985   Publication of findings from the Bristol Language Development study

LINKS

■ *How Children Learn 1*
   Vygotsky

■ *How Children Learn 2*
   Theories about how children
   learn to talk

■ *How children learn 3*
   Hughes

His life

While undertaking the language project Gordon Wells was based at Bristol University. He subsequently left, spending ten years at the University of Toronto in Canada. He is now based at the University of California Santa Cruz where he is Professor of Education. His website entry suggests that his interests are vintage cars and gardening (http://people.ucsc.edu/-gwells)

His writing

Gordon Wells is a prolific writer - a great deal of his writing is in the form of chapters in edited books. In 1985 he published the findings of the Bristol study in a book entitled *Language at Home and at School*. It is actually the second volume with that title. Volume 1 was published in 1981 and was an account of the study's methodology. These were by no means 'easy-reads' but in 1987, he published *The Meaning-Makers* which is much more accessible.

While at Toronto, Wells wrote a number of books on his continuing research interests in the role of language and dialogue in teaching and learning. Probably the best-known of these is entitled *Dialogic inquiry: towards a sociocultural practice and theory of education*. While the Bristol study was focused on the early years, his subsequent writing is cross-phase. While at Santa Cruz he has co-edited a book with Guy Claxton (see *How Children Learn 2* page 68-9 and this book page 15) entitled *Learning for life in the C21st: Sociocultural perspectives on the future of education*.

His theory

In Wells' early work, the development of language was the focus of his research. His findings from the Bristol research were published shortly after that of Tizard and Hughes (1984; see page28 of this book) and confirmed some of their findings but challenged others. His study was a very robust one - a large sample of 128 children studied over a period of more than two years. The main aspect of his theory arising from this research was that language learning was an act of social construction in which children and adults worked together. It was not something which could be explicitly taught but which developed from rewarding interactions.

In the *Meaning Makers*, Wells attempts to make his findings more accessible. He states that research is a story and that the researcher or 'story teller' weaves the best story they can from their available evidence, creating their theory in the process. Wells extends this idea to underline his view that language is the root of learning. He writes:

> We are the meaning makers - every one of us: children, parents, and teachers. To try to make sense, to construct stories, and to share them with others in speech and in writing is an essential part of being human. For those of us who are more knowledgeable and more mature - the responsibility is clear: to interact with those in our care in such a way as to foster and enrich their meaning making.
>
> (page 222)

In his later work, this theme continues (2001 page 340). He suggests that learners 'need to be treated like sense-makers rather than remembers and forgetters. They need to see connections between what they are supposed to be learning in school and things they care about understanding outside of school, and these connections need to be related to the substance of what they are supposed to be learning.'

In other research undertaken while he was in Canada, Wells draws on and develops the work of two important theorists. The first was Halliday, who a decade before the publication of Well's Bristol findings, had produced a seminal text on language development in which he links language and learning. Wells quotes Halliday as saying:

When children learn language, they are not simply engaging in one type of learning among many; rather they are learning the foundations of learning itself. The distinctive characteristic of human learning is that it is a process of making meaning.

The second major theory that Wells draws on is that of Vygotsky (see *How Children Learn* page 39). He describes himself, as Vygotsky is described as a social constructivist and writes that he had initially wanted to call his book *Dialogic Inquiry*, 'Thinking with Vygotsky'. His theories are very much in tune with those of Vygotsky's and it is this which has led him to a core element of his current theories.

Wells highlights his view that for him, knowledge is constructed when people do things together. Knowledge arises out of action; it is created between people, and it occurs as humans try to share or make meaning. We can only understand another's point of view when we actively engage. Wells, like many other theorists covered in this book (see for example Mary Jane Drummond) upholds that this act of creating meaning, like creating stories, involves the use of the imagination.

Putting the theory into practice

Although Wells early work was often difficult to read, in his later work he focuses much more on practical issues. His mission is without doubt to get adults to:

a)   support language development more effectively, and
b)   develop more collaborative practice
c)   work in more cross-curricular ways
d)   become action researchers.

Supporting language development requires that adults :
treat what children say as of value, worth listening to;
do their best to understand not just the words but the meaning;
base what they say on what the child has just said; and
use language and structures which the child can understand.

Developing collaborative practice involves seeing classrooms and other early years settings as learning communities - working towards shared goals. This should involve adults in providing:

■   Purposeful activities which involve whole persons. Wells' phrase although not intended to be specific to young children echoes the focus of early childhood education on the whole child as well as on activities are particular to the context but also unique. Although children use familiar resources the way in which activities are played out - depending on the children involved and other factors such as external events or additional stimuli: curriculum is a means not an end. 'Covering' or 'delivering' the curriculum should not be thought of as the ultimate goal of education. Wells suggests

that the knowledge and skills that make up the prescribed curriculum are a means of developing the whole person.

■   Outcomes are both aimed for and emergent. Outcomes of activity cannot be completely known or prescribed in advance; while there may be prior agreement about the goal to be aimed for, the route that is taken depends upon emergent properties of the situation.

■   Activities must allow diversity and originality: Development involves "rising above oneself", both for individuals and communities. Solving new problems requires diversity and originality of possible solutions. Without novelty, there would be no development; both individuals and societies would be trapped in an endless recycling of current activities, with all their limitations.

Working in cross-curricular ways is, for Wells, a direct result of thinking about dialogic inquiry. He cites the work of Dewey (see How Children Learn page 21) who suggests, for example, that "you can concentrate the history of all mankind into the evolution of the flax, cotton and wool fibers into clothing"(The school and society page 21-2). For Wells (and Dewey) investigations which begin with first-hand exploration of familiar aspects of the children's experience are effective because children are given real motives for doing real things. Wells goes on to highlight the importance of 'real' questions, since they are an expression of wanting to know or understand. The topic of 'real things' is also emphasised with reference to Rogoff's writing (see page 62 in this book) when Wells suggests that practical activity is essential to understanding. Reality helps children to make the connections essential to learning.

Becoming an action researcher. Wells suggests that this is essential since it offers a model of an enquiring mind. Once one encourages students to make connections between the curricular material and their own experiences, one quickly finds that they ask questions to which one does not have ready answers.

Develops collaborative learning as the learning community works together.

His influence

In the 1980s when Wells' language research was first published he had a strong influence. This is not often specifically acknowledged but in fact he continues to play a strong role in highlighting the role of language in learning. Similarly, his writing has over many years reflected views which are now given increasing recognition such as the need to develop sustained shared thinking in young children. In Dialogic inquiry, he argues that:

The purpose that currently drives public education – efficient training of young people to fit the needs of the economy – is not only severely limited as an education for full participation in a democratic society, as Dewey argued a century ago. It is also ineffective in nurturing students' development as self-directed learners and in encouraging them to collaborate in knowledge building in order to solve real-life problems of a practical as well as intellectual nature. Like many other educators, we believe that a radical change is required in the organization of public schooling and that this will best be achieved, first, by helping teachers to understand how the new ideas about learning and teaching can be brought to bear on the ways in which the curriculum is planned and enacted and, second, by persuading those in administrative positions to assist teachers in exploring new ways of teaching through collaborating with their peers in finding out about what other teachers have learned and through their own classroom-based research.

Comment

Criticisms of Wells' theories generally belong to writers and thinkers who regard learning as owing most to what is taught. As a social constructivist Wells' emphasis is firmly on the way in which children learn from others and within communities of learners.

Points for reflection

- What do you think Wells meant in referring to learners rather than rememberers and forgetters? What does this mean for practice?

References

Language Development in the Pre-school Years. (*Language at Home and at School, Vol 2*.) Gordon Wells (Cambridge University Press 1985)
Language, Learning and Education Gordon Wells (NFER-Nelson 1985)
The Meaning Makers: Children learning language and using language to learn. Gordon Wells, (Heinemann Educational Books 1986)
Dialogic inquiry: Towards a sociocultural practice and theory of education Gordon Wells (Cambridge University Press 1999)
Action, talk, and text: Learning and teaching through inquiry. Gordon Wells (ed.) (Teachers College Press 2001)
Learning for life in the C21st: Sociocultural perspectives on the future of education Gordon Wells and Guy Claxton, (eds.) (Blackwell Publishers 2002)

Where to find out more
Language Development in the Pre-school Years (Language at Home and at School, Vol 2) Gordon Wells (Cambridge University Press 1985)
http://people.ucsc.edu/~gwells/

Margy Whalley

Her life

Margy Whalley is currently Director of the Research, Development and Training Base at the Pen Green Centre and is involved in research, training and consultancy work in this country and Europe, New Zealand and Australia. She has managed multi-disciplinary early years services in Brazil, Papua New Guinea and England. She was the founding Head of the Pen Green Centre for Under 5s and their families and has worked there since 1983. Margy has received an MBE award in honour of her outstanding contribution to childcare development over the past 35 years and in 2005 she received a Lifetime Achievement Award.

She has an MA in Community Education and a PhD on Leadership in Integrated Centres. She undertook a secondment to the Open University where she wrote course materials for parents wanting to increase their knowledge and understanding of child development.

She was invited to be part of the Labour Party's enquiry team into Under 5s education and care and was the Association of County Council's representative on the National Audit commission concerned with children under five. Margy was heavily involved in the development of the Early Excellence Centre programme and was responsible for piloting and developing the National Professional Qualification in Integrated Centre Leadership programme. She was on the advisory board of the National Early Excellence Evaluation programme and the Early Years Advisory Group for the Department for Education and Skills (DfES).

Her writing

Involving Parents in their Children's Learning was first published in 2000 and is now in its second edition. She has also written two other books on the subject of partnership with parents - *Learning to be strong* which was published in 1994 and *Working with Parents*, published three years later. Margy Whalley has also written a range of materials on leadership and management, including those for the National Professional Qualification in Integrated Centre Leadership (NPQICL) and for the Open University.

Her research and theory

The primary function of the research programme over the last 5 years has been involving parents in their children's learning programme and developing a leadership learning route for those leading integrated centres, such as children's centres. These two areas represent the heart of Margy's philosophy.

Since she first opened the centre Margy Whalley has shown continued commitment to recognition and development of the crucial contribution which parents can make to children's development when professionals enter into genuine partnership with them. Pen Green has without doubt been in the vanguard of practice becoming not merely one of the first Early Excellence centres identified by the government but virtually setting the template for those that followed. Now more than 500 families use the open-access centre every week, and more than 6,000 parents have taken part in the centre's pioneering partnership programme since it opened.

In 1996 Pen Green set up a research base in partnership with parents, staff and researchers at the University of Northampton. On the website of Research in Practice (www.rip.org.uk) Margy Whalley explains the work of the centre in developing partnership:

Research has shown that a large number of parents want to be involved in their children's early school experiences, and also indicates that children gain when their parents are involved in early childhood programmes. But researchers were still unclear about precisely how parental involvement actually benefited children in nursery settings. At Pen Green we wanted to develop a partnership with parents where we could explore this process and come to a clearer understanding of the contribution parents were making.

She continues:

Our image of the child is rich in potential, strong, powerful, competent and most of all connected to the adults and other children around them. We wanted to build on parents' competencies, not their deficiencies, and recognise the crucial role they play in educating their children.

From the outset, parents are encouraged to watch for and understand schema (see *How Children Learn 1* page 50; and the section on Tina Bruce in this, book page 12) in their children's behaviour, which show how the child tries to understand the world. Tina Bruce was for many years the pedagogue at Pen Green, guiding staff in their understanding of schema. She was followed in this role by Chris Athey. Both have supported staff in developing their role in relation to children and parents.

The second key strand of Whalley's theory has emerged since the creation of the Pen Green Research Base in 1995. The establishment of this base has enabled Margy Whalley to train practitioners as leaders, using an experiential approach. Initially an MA in Care and Education was set up but, over time, more courses have been developed, accredited with a range of universities. Most notable has been the development of the NPQICL.

Putting the theory into practice

One of the most influential strategies employed at Pen Green to involve parents has been work involving videoing children. Parents borrow video cameras to film their children at the centre and at home, and are offered training in what to look for as they observe their children learn. They are invited to attend workshops and study groups on child development at a variety of times to suit the needs of all parents, including those who are working shifts. Parents and staff share their observations and discuss the possible next steps for each child.

Pen Green has a passionate commitment to believing that almost all parents want to help their children learn. Belief in parents has had an impact not only on children's learning and development but also in parents' confidence and enthusiasm for extending their own learning.

At a conference (23/3/09 www.childrens-centres.org) Margy Whalley emphasised the importance both of engaging fathers and of taking account of the real difficulties that parents face and finding ways to support them. She also suggested that effective practice in engaging children and families involves:

- 'Encouraging families to participate in the re-shaping of the shared context in which they live out their individual lives
- Supporting parents and children to become effective public service users
- Building the capacity of children, families and communities to secure outcomes for themselves
- Harnessing the community's energy for change and parent's deep commitment to ensuring that their children have a better deal.'

Her influence

In the newsletter of the Childcare Recruitment Campaign for July 2005, Anne Longfield, Chief Executive of 4Children described Margy Whalley as "a pioneer, a leader, a published author, well respected in local as well as central Government and someone who has an incredible CV. She is also highly regarded by the children, families and colleagues she works with and .... is a truly caring, dedicated and inspirational individual."

Her passion is clear in all she does - transforming the lives of children and families through change. In this she has been highly influential in political and professional circles - pioneering integrated centres and developing practice which firmly incorporates partnership with parents.

Comment

The concept of Early Excellence centres and Children's Centres, which Margy Whalley has pioneered, has been criticised as being costly and giving a small number of settings large sums of money while leaving the majority of providers with much less to spend. This view has been countered by suggesting that without trailblazing schemes of this sort nothing would change.

NPQICL has been criticised as offering a narrow one-sided view of leadership. In line with Margy's philosophy it focuses on transformative leadership (that is, leadership which focuses on transforming or improving people's lives, rather than merely managing aspects of an organisation) and places a strong emphasis on experiential learning - learning through experiences and doing, rather than listening and 'being told'. Counter-arguments have included the suggestion that leadership in the early years requires particular qualities. While it may share some characteristics with other forms of leadership and management, the fact that it involves dealing with society's youngest and most vulnerable members means that it has some idiosyncratic qualities as well.

Points for reflection

- Do you think that some Children's Centres have been over-funded at the expense of other settings? Or do you agree that creating opportunities for ground-breaking innovation improves provision overall?

References

www.childrens-centres.org
Involving parents in their children's learning Margy Whalley (Paul Chapman Publishing 2007/2nd ed)
Learning to be strong Margy Whalley (Hodder Arnold 1994)
Working with Parents Margy Whalley and the Pen Green Team (Hodder Educational 1997)

Where to find out more
www.pengreen.org.uk
www.CREC.co.uk

Brain and body

The development of neuroscientific understanding has added weight to the importance of physical action in relation to the development of the brain.

- *How Children Learn 1*
  Research into brain development
  Piaget
  Athey
  Bruner
  Gardner

- *How Children Learn 3*
  Claxton

Some key thinking and ideas about brain and body

Far from being separate parts of the human being (or animal), brain and body are entirely dependent on one another. Professor Susan Greenfield has written that "you only need a brain when you are moving. For stationary life forms, a brain is no longer necessary" (1997 page 34). Studies of development have long-emphasised the links:

Piaget and sensorimotor learning

At the time that Piaget was developing his theories there was much less hard evidence about the workings of brain and body but Piaget was a biologist by training and perhaps it was this that led him to an understanding of the relationship between thought and action. Piaget's theories were taken up and developed by Chris Athey who applied schema theory in her analysis of children's representations of their experience. In writing about schema, Athey identifies physical action as the first stage of exploring individual schema.

Piaget maintained that the sensorimotor stage of learning went on throughout the first two years of life and that after that children moved on to what he termed the pre-operational, concrete operational and finally the formal operational stages of thinking and learning.

Bruner

Bruner also saw the early stages of learning as related to physical action. The major difference lies in the fact that for Piaget, development was a one-way street. Once you had gone through the sensorimotor stage, you never went back there. For Bruner, what he terms the 'enactive' or initial mode of learning is the starting point whenever we meet something new.

Gardner and bodily-kinaesthetic intelligence

Howard Gardner initially wrote about Multiple Intelligence Theory in 1983. He identified bodily-kinaesthetic intelligence as one of six or eight intelligences and wrote about "languages of the body". Many writers have subsequently identified a kinaesthetic learning style but Gardner himself does not support this idea. Practitioners working with young children should perhaps pay special attention to this, since labelling young children as particular kinds of learners has many dangers. All young children need to explore through touch, movement, sound and vision. In the foundation years, children are laying pathways in the brain which will be the foundation of all future learning.

Five senses, six senses or more?

Since the time of Aristotle it has been widely stated that humans have five senses - namely sight; hearing; touch; smell; and taste. In everyday conversation people regularly refer to our sixth sense or clairvoyant powers. Steiner education suggests that there are twelve senses, divided into will, soul and spiritual senses.

In the second half of the twentieth century, a further sense known as proprioception came to the fore. This is the sense which allows you to know your body's position and movement in space (sometimes referred to as kinaesthesia). Since then these ideas have been extended. Blakeslee and Blakeslee (2007) refer to flesh-bound (or somatic) senses, which they suggest enable our brains to map what is called our peripersonal space. Our brains apparently include in the map, the tools or spaces we are using. So for example, when we are gardening or sweeping, our sense of peripersonal space goes right down to the end of the tool we are holding. It is also the reason why we duck when our car goes under a low bridge - we have a sense that the car is part of us! Blakeslee and Blakeslee include in these flesh-bound senses, touch and proprioception, but also refer to:

- thermoception (the sense of heat or its absence)
- nocioception (the sense of pain), and

balance (often referred to as the vestibular sense, or equilibrioception).

Brain and body/ body and brain

Lise Eliot (1999) reminds us that scientific interest in babies' earliest movements has only developed recently. In the first half of the twentieth century it was still widely believed that the development of motor skills was inborn and that practice therefore made little difference to the rate of development.

However, later neuroscientific studies (based on Eliot 1999 page 276) have found that:

- Babies do improve their motor skills much as adults do - as a result of diligent practice. New skills such as walking independently don't suddenly emerge out of nowhere but gradually build out of prior, simpler abilities - kicking, standing and walking with support - after weeks or months of trying.

- Adults and babies learn in similar ways but, for babies, practice only works when their brains are maturationally ready. In other words, practice is essential, provided it's done at the right time. Done too early, the necessary circuits simply aren't there to benefit from it. (Indeed some researchers believe that premature practice can actually interfere with the acquisition of certain skills, either because it ends up training the wrong neural pathways or because the baby grows frustrated with trying to do something he has no hope of mastering at the time.)

Mirror neurons

It was not until the late 1990s that mirror neurons were identifed. Colwyn Trevarthen calls them 'empathy neurons', while Ramachandran refers to them as 'monkey-see, monkey do neurons'. An Italian, Rizzolatti,

discovered that when a monkey watches another monkey, for example, grabbing a peanut the same firing pattern occurs in their brains - whether actually grabbing the peanut or just observing. The same thing happens in human adults - when you watch someone playing tennis or dancing, your brain produces the same firing pattern - unfortunately not the same calorie loss or muscle tone but the same action in parts of the brain.

This also occurs in new-born babies. When an adult smiles or pokes his or her tongue out at the baby, the baby will (given time and being awake) imitate the adult's action. It appears that young children need to imitate as a vital aspect of learning so nothing inhibits them from behaving as the mirror neurons dictate. As they get older (and in adulthood) we become better able to control the urge to imitate and can confine it to our heads. (Yawning may be an exception - when someone yawns most people feel the urge to copy - but this may be because the lack of oxygen or overheating which caused the first yawn contributes to the subsequent imitations.)

Putting the theory into practice

This vast area of research and theory has many implications for practice. Listed below are some of them:

- Physical exercise has an important role to play in providing the right conditions for the brain to thrive.
- Physical exploration provides the foundation for future thinking and enables the brain to make a wealth of connections. Active learning does not have to be physical - it really refers to active engagement but learning does rely on physical action and exploration.
- There is a strong link between learning and the senses. Vestibular action, for example, (which includes all the

rocking, twisting and turning upside down) stimulates the brain. This and others of these points argue for provision which allows young children to be physically active at a time and manner of their choosing.

- Playful activity is essential to learning and development. Children spend longer practising or rehearsing when they are able to set the pace and frequency. Think about a baby learning to stand - they practise for long periods - are much more demanding of themselves than we would be. Time and space can once again be seen to be vital ingredients of learning.
- The existence of mirror neurons is said to offer strong support for the integration of children with special needs. They can learn from the actions of other children the things that might otherwise inhibit their progress. So for example, a child unable to climb can develop some spatial awareness by watching an able-bodied child climb.
- Mirror neurons also show that imitation is a vital part of learning. Copying the actions of others should not be seen as a negative but as children finding out what that feels like. Without good imitational abilities, many things would be very difficult to learn.

The influence of developing theories about brain and body

Brain studies have had a powerful impact on our understanding of learning and development. We are all endlessly fascinated by what our brains can do and are frequently aghast at what scientists are discovering about human abilities. It is difficult to keep up with the changes in knowledge and perhaps even more difficult to interpret what they mean for practice.

Comment

Practitioners need to be careful about taking on the implications of these ideas. Claxton (2008) comments in no uncertain terms about "hints and tips (that) come with impressive-sounding justifications in terms of 'brain-friendly learning'". He gives three reasons for his scepticism:

- Neuroscience is in its infancy and findings may easily turn out to be flawed.
- It is not clear that the 'brain-friendly learning' techniques actually work. He is particularly scathing about work on learning styles.
- Many of the hints and tips are "too insignificant to provide the foundation for a renewed purpose for education as a whole". In his view what is needed are sustained attempts to develop children's confidence through curiosity, resilience, imagination and reflection.

One of the techniques which has been widely taken up in the early years is Brain Gym. Much of what has been written in this section should cause practitioners who are using it to review their practice, asking themselves questions such as:

- How do I know that this is the right time for this particular child to be doing this?
- How do I know that this will be effective (or any more effective than play situations which support children in developing a wide range of movements)? A recent American study suggested that the only movement which really required particular provision was brachiating (moving by hanging from your arms as you do on monkey bars).

As Claxton points out neuroscientific explanations and theories are constantly changing. Forty years ago, for example, it was not believed that new born babies could smile in response to someone smiling. The advent of video cameras together with the discovery of mirror neurons has rendered that view completely wrong.

In the early days of neuroscience 'hot housing' or accelerating learning, was regarded as desirable. The emphasis placed on formal learning by policy makers and some parents echoes that view. However, it is becoming increasingly clear that, as in Lilian Katz's words "just because children can do something doesn't mean they should". Tobin reminds us that these pressures create "an imbalance which favours the brain over the body and skill acquisition over feelings and more complex thinking".

Points for reflection
- What might be the value of imitation in human learning?
- What are the implications of babies' apparent need to train themselves at the appropriate point in their development?

References
The Body has a Mind of its own Sandra and Matthew Blakeslee (Random House 2007)
Early Intelligence: how the brain and mind develop in the first five years of life Lise Eliot, (Penguin Books 1999)
The Human Brain: a guided tour Susan Greenfield, (Weidenfeld and Nicolson 1997) :
What's the point of school? Guy Claxton (One World 2008)

Where to find out more
Knowing Bodies, Moving Minds: towards embodied teaching and learning Liora Bresler (ed) (Kluwer Academic Publishers 2004) (see especially chapters 6 and 7)
Breadth and depth in early foundations' In Fisher, J. (ed) *The Foundations of Learning* Linda Pound, (Open University Press 2002)

Some key thinking and theories about the care and education of babies and toddlers

Theories about babies have changed across centuries. This is reflected in Christina Hardyment's book *Dream Babies*. The latest edition (published in 2007) is subtitled 'childcare advice from John Locke to Gina Ford'. The earlier edition published more than twenty years ago, in 1983, was subtitled 'childcare from Locke to Spock'.

The plethora of theories also vary from culture to culture. This is reflected in a book entitled *A world of babies: imagined childcare guides for seven societies*. In his introduction to the book (page ix), Jerome Bruner writes:

There is nothing in the world to match child rearing for the depth and complexity of the challenges it poses both for those directly caught up in its daily intricacies and for the society to which child and caretakers belong...... And it is not only prolonged helplessness that is special about human infancy, but its utter reliance on sustained and extended interaction with a committed and acculturated caregiver.

Both of the books referred to make it clear that there is no one right way. And yet we all hold very strong views about what the right way is. There is probably no role on earth with greater

PROFILE

Understandings of child psychology and development over the last twenty years have transformed views of what babies know and can do. Yet anxieties persist, and have perhaps even increased about whether adults are doing the right thing.

LINKS

- *How Children learn 1*
  Bowlby
  Research into brain development

- *How children learn 2*
  How children learn to talk

- *How children learn 3*
  Abbott
  Belsky
  Trevarthen
  Brain and body

responsibility for the future of society as well as each individual than practitioners caring for children up to the age of three. Such young children are at their most vulnerable and arguably at their most malleable. No other workers are at the same time beleaguered by the views of parents, society, politicians and the person in the street. The views put forward in this section are Eurocentric and cannot possibly reflect the full range of practice. It can (and does, I hope) draw attention to the rich diversity and consider ways of trying to understand different approaches and views.

There is another aspect to be considered. Alison James and her colleagues suggest that the term 'babyhood' did not come into use until the period at the end of the nineteenth century and the early part of the twentieth century. The same concern which motivated the MacMillan sisters to set up nurseries, develop school meals and campaign for the introduction of school nurses led to a public health campaign and the appointment of an army of health visitors. During this period infant mortality was drastically reduced and, argues Alison James, families began to regard babyhood as having significance for life.

Learning from observation
Throughout time, there has been interest in what babies do. This section will consider the impact of observation.

Baby biographies in the eighteenth and nineteenth centuries. In 1744, Pestalozzi published his observations of his three-year-old son. Darwin published observations of one of his sons in 1877. Their close observations shaped their views and can thus be seen as being of great importance in our understanding of development.

The child study movement in the twentieth century. Darwin's work stimulated interest in child study. Throughout the twentieth century a number of famous parents wrote child studies of their own children. Piaget is perhaps the most notable example but there are others. Ruth Weir studied her child's vocalisations in the cot. Dorothy Butler wrote two memorable books based on her granddaughter's experience of books. More recently Cath Arnold of Pen Green has written about her grandson. These books are powerful because observers who know the children well are noting and interpreting what they see. (For more about this see Bartholomew and Bruce chapter 2.)

Listening in the twenty-first century. In the twenty first century there has been considerable interest in listening to children. This idea has grown out of concern for children's rights but it has raised issues about how you listen to children who are too young (or not able) to speak. This has led to the development of the idea that babies' intentions or meanings can be interpreted from observing them closely. (For more about this see *Young Children's Health and Well-being* and *Beyond Listening*.)

Learning from research
Research into the development of babies and toddlers has been facilitated by video camera. There continues to be widespread interest in how babies develop and their apparently immense capabilities. Tom Bower, writing and researching in the 1970s, was amongst the first to awaken public interest to the competence of very young children - particularly in problem-solving. Colwyn Trevarthen has led the way in demonstrating the social nature of infants. Dan Siegel has alerted us to the relationship between cognition and sociability. These and numerous other researchers, theorists and thinkers have contributed to our understanding of babies and toddlers.

We should not forget, however, that alongside this growth of research and knowledge into development, the changing fortunes of Bowlby's theories. When Bowlby published his findings after the end of the second world war, there was political and social influence to accept his ideas. In the 1970s and 1980s, many women came to regard his theories as being anti-feminist and nursery services were seen by many as needing to place the mother and family (rather than the child) at the centre of their thinking. Many continue to hold this view but recent research has caused some people to question whether group care settings can meet the needs of babies and toddlers (see for example the section in this book on Belsky page 6). While this has not meant a widespread return to thinking that mothers must stay at home, it has led many to focus on the quality of group settings for babies and very young children.

Putting the theory into practice
In this section the focus will be on *Meeting the Needs of Children from Birth to Three*, published by the Scottish Government. This document is, as the full title suggests (see reference section below), concerned with attempting to put the theory into practice. The document sets out the provision required for babies and toddlers. Each section is summarised and it is the summaries that are shown below:

For infants under one year of age:
- Consistent care giving by one adult or a very small number of adults able to form a warm relationship with the child and to respond sensitively to the infants' changing needs and preferences and developing pride in achievement;
- Minimising staff turnover and changes of carers;
- A focus on responding to infants as individuals with their own needs;
- Communication about the changing ways and temperaments of babies with parents...

During the second year of life provision should offer:
- A consistent relationship with a caregiver who knows the child's stage of cognitive, linguistic, social and emotional development well;

- Adults who are ready and able to interact with children in talk, imitative behaviour, discovery and pretend play;
- A social environment rich in opportunities to develop language, symbolic coding and classifying, movement and engagement with music, rhyme and creativity;
- Sensitivity to the social and cultural background of the child and opportunities for parents and caregivers to share their understanding of the child...

During the third year of life provision should offer:

- Opportunities to express and represent discoveries and learning in different media;
- Imaginative and inventive play and discovery in groups, alone and with interested adults;
- Adults who are aware of each child's stage of development in language, social competence, cognition and moral reasoning and who are able to share and lead the infant's discoveries and their participation in the world of older children and adults;
- Attention to each child's sense of well-being, self-worth and pride in achievement.

The influence of theories about the care and education of babies and toddlers

Our individual theories about the care and education of babies and toddlers are so much a part of our unconscious thinking that external reports and views cannot always be readily absorbed. We all need time to take on new ideas, but change is and does happen. In particular the research about babies' competence is very persuasive and interesting. (See for example *How Babies Think*.)

Comment

Some sources of criticism come from postmodern deconstructionist theorists, such as Erica Burman who believes that researchers are simply constructing babies as competent and social. They challenge the views of researchers such as Trevarthen (see page 59 of this book).

There is widespread criticism in this country of approaches such as *Letters and Sounds* (DfES 2007). This is against a background where many practitioners are increasingly worried about an over-formalisation of learning, too much too soon. The focus on phonic knowledge prior to the introduction of the Every Child a Talker Project; the focus on areas of learning and development which include numeracy and literacy for babies and toddlers are seen as unnecessary, unhelpful and unwonted intrusions into infancy. Hence, some newspapers have ridiculed the document. The Daily Mail for example carried the headline "Babies assessed on babbling and gurgling".

Points for reflection

- If you work with children up to the age of three how far are you able to put theory into practice? What makes this difficult? What could be done to improve practice?
- How far do you think group care settings can cater for very young children?
- How do you think the Scottish guidance compares with the EYFS or other curriculum frameworks you have used?

References

A world of babies: imagined childcare guides for seven societies Judy DeLoache and Alma Gottlieb (Cambridge University Press 2000)
Beyond Listening edited by Alison Clark et al (Policy Press 2005)
Dream babies: childcare advice from John Locke to Gina Ford Christina Hardyment (Oxford University Press 2007)
Early Years Foundation Stage
How Babies Think Alison Gopnik et al (1999 Weidenfeld and Nicolson)
Letters and Sounds DfES 2007
Meeting the needs of children from birth to three: research evidence and implications for out-of-home provision Christine Stephen, Aline-Wendy Dunlop, Colwyn Trevarthen and Helen Markwick (The Scottish Government 2003) Obtainable on-line www.scotland. gov.uk/Publications/2003/06/17458/22696
Theorizing childhood Alison James et al (Polity Press 2005)
Young Children's Health and Well-being Angela Underdown (Open University Press 2007)

Where to find out more
Key Times for Play: A framework for developing high quality provision for children from birth to three Julia Manning-Morton and Maggie Thorp (Open University Press 2006)
Key Times for Play: The first three years Julia Manning-Morton and Maggie Thorp (Open University Press 2003)

Gender issues- educating boys and girls

Some key thinking and theories about gender

The key to understanding research about boys and girls is the nature/ nurture debate. Evolutionary psychologists, such as Steven Pinker, are likely to take a firm line on gender differences being the result of millions of years of evolution and therefore part of our nature. Those who argue that gender differences are natural point to the higher levels of dopamine, testosterone and vasopressin found in boys. They highlight too the greater blood flow found in the brains of boys and its link to physical action. Girls, on the other hand, are found to have better connections between the two halves of their brains and an earlier development of parts of the cerebral cortex.

The value of such findings is challenged. Penny Holland highlights research which shows for example that testosterone levels may not be the cause of aggression, but the result of aggressive activity. She cites neuroscientist Susan Greenfield and points out that as we find out just how sophisticated and flexible our brains are "the balance between nature and nurture seems to swing in favour of nurture" (Holland, 2003, page 17)

Social constructivists such as Barbara Rogoff are likely to suggest that the culture in which children grow up (or in other words how they are nurtured) accounts for gender differences. Rogoff (2003) argues, for example, that girls are given more guidance in 'proper social behaviour' than boys and that different tasks are usually assigned to children depending on whether they are boys or girls. In support of her argument, she cites practices in the Luo community in Kenya. In this example, although chores are usually assigned on a gender basis, where there is no older daughter, boys may be required to look after younger siblings. Those who have such experience were found to be less aggressive, more pro-social and generally more caring than those who had only taken on traditional roles.

Those who regard gender as being mainly about human nature suggest that the fact that training has little or no impact in changing behaviour amongst men and women, underlines the fact that we are fighting nature. Rogoff on the other hand suggests that children construct the stereotypes from messages we hardly know we're sending. She writes:

> *Children look for regularities in behaviour based on salient categories in their community. Gender is invariably a salient category.... They look for rules, and if they think they have found one, they are more narrow about its application than their elders, often overlooking examples to the contrary. (page 75)*

She gives the example of one of her own daughters seeing two suited men on the television and asking what they were. When told they were professors, the child replied that they couldn't be because they were men. The only professor she knew was a woman, her mother. Similarly two-year old Edward saw a picture of someone with a stethoscope. He asked what the person was doing and was told that it was a doctor. His reply, despite the fact that his family doctor was a woman, was "she can't be a doctor, he's wearing lipstick!" The confusion over pronouns underlines his sense of confusion about the cultural rules.

Rogoff continues:

> *Subtle information about gender in young children's daily lives may be especially likely to be taken for granted..... Patterns that are perceived without conscious awareness or without being pointed out are especially likely to be regarded subsequently as preferable and more pleasant.....for this reason, gender roles ... (are) quite resilient and slow to change. (page 76)*

Putting the theory into practice

Holland (2003 page 19) reminds us that young children are 'struggling to make sense of what it means to be a boy or a girl'. They are 'in the process of forming gender identity.... trying to find ...rules that will make them feel that they belong in the gendered world that surrounds them'.

Practitioners are also struggling. Parents views may differ radically from those held by practitioners and practitioners themselves may find it difficult to reconcile their personal beliefs about gender with those of others around them. Yet it is clear that children are absorbing views that we are not even aware of transmitting, so we have an important task not to limit children's life chances by promoting stereotypical behaviour.

The key to resolving this is to ensure that what we do as practitioners supports children educationally. This will have benefits for all children because in the midst of nature/ nurture debates it's important to remember that the differences between one boy and another or one girl and another are greater than the differences between boys and girls as a whole!

Supporting boys **and** girls is most likely to be effective when we:

- **Create communication -friendly environments.** Since boys' communication skills and interest in literacy is said to be less-well developed than those of girls, this is vital. Making time and space for sustained, shared conversations and creating lots of opportunities for small group interactions - with and without adults will help. It's also vital to check that while modelling language use, you're not hogging too much of the available space. There should be a balance - if you're doing more of the talking than anyone else you need to rethink

- **Support positive learning dispositions.** It's important to recognise that attitudes and habits such as perseverance, persistence, taking responsibility or communicating are vital to all learning and they should be nurtured. But we should remember that things like risk-taking (stereotypically a male behaviour) are of great value.

- **Ensure warm environments that promote a sense of security.** Some researchers (see for example Gurian) argue that boys need a greater sense of attachment to educators. This will involve adults in:
  - giving attention for positive behaviour and activities;
  - verbally mirroring what children are doing and joining in with their play;
  - following children's lead and interests;
  - being enthusiastic, predictable and consistent.

- **Promoting children's sense of independence and opportunities for making choices.** It is often noted that girls wander less and that this has an impact on their spatial awareness and, in the longer-term, their mathematical ability. Similarly it is suggested that boys seem to value a sense of freedom. Being warned about changes in activity - such as clearing up time - and being given the opportunity to make decisions wherever possible can support this.

The influence of theories about gender

Since the 1970s there has been a tidal flow of publications and research studies about the impact of gender on achievement, attitudes and behaviour. It is interesting to note Rogoff's comment that we are more comfortable with patterns of behaviour which do

War, weapon and superhero play in the early years

This is the subtitle to Penny Holland's book We don't play with guns here. Penny's research focused on what she terms the 'zero tolerance' for gun and weapon play in early childhood settings. Her theory is that by effectively banning what appears to be a principle interest of boys in superheroes and all that entails we are alienating them from learning. She suggests that practitioners should allow gun play providing they are guns or weapons created from construction sets of found materials. Replica weapons should not be used. By allowing this play, children are enabled to develop and transform it. Holland concludes her book with a quote from Vivian Gussin Paley:

If I have not yet learned to love Darth Vader, I have at least made some useful discoveries while watching him at play. As I interrupt less, it becomes clear that boys' play is serious drama, not morbid mischief. Its rhythms and images are often discordant to me, but I must try to make sense of a style that, after all, belongs to half the population of the classroom.

Gender issues- educating boys and girls

not challenge us or which are less than conscious. This means that comments or actions which challenge our views are not comfortable and we tend to retreat from them.

Views on gender are changing, but for many people the rate of change is too slow. This does not mean that they are not having an influence. You might also consider the view that change occurs because of extreme views that are voiced. Society might not like them but they make it easier to take on moderate change.

Comment

Throughout the history of child development and psychology, many of the views expressed have been challenged on gender grounds. Freud in particular has been heavily criticised. In relation to moral development, Kohlberg has been challenged (see moral development in this book page 79) as giving greater status to male judgements than female ones. Piaget has been criticised as offering a male view of the child (see for example Burman). Bowlby was criticised for his views on attachment which seemed to demand that mothers, but not fathers, needed to be with their child throughout their early years.

More recent work which focuses on gender differences is not however above criticism. This is not surprising when it is clear that there are strongly held views on both sides of the nature vs. nurture debate. However, one criticism may be levelled at Michael Gurian in particular. He writes:

> Impulsivity used to be much more useful and desirable in learning, especially when children did more of their learning outdoors and independently (Gurian and Stevens 2005 page 49)

This is very worrying since it implies that approaches to learning can be changed at whim. As we have seen, risk-taking remains vital to learning. Conformity has been seen as the enemy of girls' achievement since it robs them of impulsivity - yet Gurian seems to be suggesting that the change he notes in teaching is acceptable. Outdoor learning and independent learning remain essential and it is the role of practitioners to ensure that children have opportunities to both be taught and to learn in these ways.

A further criticism may be addressed to those purporting to support the development of boys and girls. Featherstone and Bayley repeatedly emphasise the need for boys to have 'brain breaks'. Educators only need to offer formal 'brain breaks' if their approach to teaching and learning does not enable and trust children to gauge when they need breaks. Enforced breaks - no matter how well-meaning - can undermine concentration.

Points for reflection
- Have you (like Penny Holland and Vivian Gussin Paley) learned to love superheroes? What did you discover about boys' play?
- Have you noticed any challenges to your views on gender which have felt uncomfortable? Reflect on why this might be.

References
The Cultural Nature of Human Development, Barbara Rogoff (Oxford University Press 2003)
We don't play with guns here - war, weapon and superhero play in the early years Penny Holland (Open University Press 2003)
Boys and Girls Come Out to Play Sally Featherstone and Ros Bayley (A&C Black 2005)
The Minds of Boys Michael Gurian and Kathy Stevens (Jossey Bass 2005)

Where to find out more
Boys and girls: superheroes in the doll corner Vivian Gussin Paley (University of Chicago Press 1984)
Who's calling the shots? Nancy Carlsson Paige and Diane Levin (New Society 1990)
Boys and girls learn differently! Michael Gurian (Jossey-Bass 2001)
Racism, gender identities and young children Paul Connolly (Routledge 1998)
We don't play with guns here: war, weapon and superhero play in the early years Penny Holland (OUP 2003)

Some key thinking and theories about learning outdoors

In the eighteenth century the writings and experimental schemes of Rousseau and Pestalozzi emphasised the importance of nature and the outdoor environment. Both Robert Owen and Friedrich Froebel spent some time at Pestalozzi's boarding school and, in setting up their nursery provision in the nineteenth century, both were strongly influenced by his work.

At New Lanark, Robert Owen ensured that children spent many hours each day in the open air. Froebel devised the term 'kindergarten'. For him nursery education provided a children's garden - both in terms of a garden for children and as an environment where children would be nourished and nurtured like young plants. He was a trained forester and believed that the beauty and freedom, space and light offered by the outdoors supported children's all-round development and spirituality.

Outdoor provision in the twentieth century

The McMillan sisters set up the first nursery school in London in response to the poor health of children in Deptford. Their first initiative in the area was an outdoor night camp to improve the health of those at risk of contracting tuberculosis. The nursery school had a large garden and classrooms were described as shelters - designed simply to shelter children in bad weather. The expectation was that children would normally live and play outdoors. Margaret McMillan also set up an outdoor residential camp in Kent so that children from Deptford could experience the countryside. These developments were occurring at the same time as the Order of Woodcraft Chivalry was being established.

In the inter-war period there was a surge of innovative provision - many of which emphasised outdoor learning. In 1924, for example, Susan Isaacs set up a nursery which encouraged exploration and enquiry, particularly in the garden. This included "grass, fruit trees, a climbing frame, slides. Movable ladders, trees for climbing, flowers and vegetable gardens with individual plots for each child and a range of animals, including chickens, guinea pigs, as well as snakes and salamanders" (Tovey 2007 page 47). In 1928 the first Forest School was set up in Hampshire and in the following year the Chelsea Open-Air Nursery School was set up in London.

In the 1960s however, nursery education began to have less outdoor provision. A shortage of places led to a lowering of standards of space as playgroups and nursery classes became more prevalent. Alongside this, other factors limited children's access to fresh air and open spaces. These include:

- Less space and opportunity to play outdoors. Cars, a fear of abduction, smaller gardens and an earlier start to school have all contributed to what has been described as the incarceration of children.
- Growing intolerance of children's play. Alongside the restrictions on children's play outdoors there has been a growth in people's tolerance of play. One mother, a journalist, has written about feeling as though she was a bad parent because she allowed her children to play unsupervised outdoors. Helen Penn has suggested that children, like the skylark, have disappeared from our landscapes (cited by Tovey).
- Television and electronic toys. Too much time spent indoors watching TV etc. is regarded as a problem on a number of grounds. Damage to health (particularly the risk of obesity) and limits on thinking (see for example Greenfield 2006) are two of the perceived dangers but there is a particular developmental danger, expressed by a journalist (cited by Tovey):
  For the first time in 4 million year history of our species, we are effectively trapping children indoors at the very point when their bodies and minds are primed to start getting to grips with the world outside the home,

The traditions of early childhood education placed a strong emphasis on learning outdoors. Since that time there has been growing interest in the value of outdoor environments. The Early Years Foundation Stage guidance (2007) places a stronger emphasis on outdoor environments than previous guidance in this country.

- *How Children learn 1*
  Forest Schools

Learning outdoors

Outdoor learning in the twenty first century
Research in health, social policy and psychology has highlighted a wide range of benefits for children from playing and learning outdoors.

Developmental requirements of young children - playing outdoors enables young children to play in ways that match their developmental needs.

- It is an environment that constantly changes with the weather, time of day and seasons and these changes excite exploration, curiosity and wonder. It offers resources that can be transformed into anything you want. This rich context for play where children can use 'loose parts' (Tovey) such as stones, twigs grass and so on to stand for other things cannot be matched indoors.
- Outside it's fine to be noisy, messy and to do things on a grand scale. More space means that children are better able to be involved in the range of movement opportunities that they need to develop brain and body, thinking and the sensory experience of 'knowing your place in space'(Tovey). The mapping which goes on in the brain as children develop spatial skills and proprioception (see page 66 Brain and Body in this book) contributes to children's cognitive abilities (Risotto and Giuliani 2006 cited by Tovey).
- Young children need to be excited - excitement alters the chemistry of the brain and makes learning more effective. Being outside makes it more acceptable (and manageable) to be, to quote Helen Tovey, giddy, gleeful and dizzy. Playful learning promotes creativity and encourages children to make unusual connections and try out unusual ideas.
- The freedom offered by being outside improves health and well-being. A Swedish study found that, whatever they were doing, simply being outdoors made children twice as active as when they were indoors. Whole body movements, rough and tumble play and an environment that stimulates all the senses supports a sense of well-being and all-round physical health - enhancing the development of the brain and the central nervous system. Fresh air and natural landscapes have been shown to contribute to mental health.

Opportunities to take risks and to learn to be safe - outdoor provision encourages a willingness to take risks. This in turn promotes children's sense of 'agency' or independence. Playing outdoors allows for risky play - physically and socially. It enables children to set themselves challenges - learning in the process how to stay safe.

Developing naturalistic intelligence - Howard Gardner's work on multipleintelligences has suggested that naturalistic intelligence is of great importance. This view is echoed by Richard Louv who suggests that children today need to be protected from 'nature-deficit disorder'. He refers to naturalistic intelligence as the eighth intelligence and highlights the wide range of learning and understanding that come from being in a naturalistic environment. Outdoors children can engage with the natural world and begin to understand their place within it. Nature for the child is sheer sensory experience. It is ever-changing and yet it is predictable.

Putting the theory into practice
In order to put these theories into practice, the outdoor environme... needs to cater for:

- **Cross-curricular activity** - learning outdoors should not be confined to physical development or scientific understanding but should cater for all aspects of provision. Helen Bilton's books give good guidance on setting up areas of provision. Helen Tovey suggests that while you need to pay attention to a full range of provision it is also important to allow for flexibility so that children can make connections between areas of learning and provision. Jan White includes chapters on using natural materials, playing with water, imaginative play and construction.

- **Developmental needs** - practitioners need to check that there are opportunities for children to be noisy, messy and giddy. There also need to be lots of 'loose parts' (Tovey) - materials that children can move about, mix together and explore fully. The outside area, no matter how small, needs features against which children can map where they are in relation to other things - bushes, flower pots, markings and so on. Children also need tools - brooms, spades and vehicles against which they can map their bodies within the environment.
- **Developing independence** - The current over-emphasis on avoiding risk is harming children (see for example *Toxic Childhood*). Children need to take risks if they are to learn to stay safe. Sue Palmer writes for example: " children no longer experience.... 'everyday adventures', those small but significant experiences through which they learn about the world, develop their physical coordination and control, and grow in independence. Everyday adventures are an unpredictable but essential part of growing up - they are opportunities to make judgements, take risks, learn how to make friends and elude enemies. But they depend upon the freedom to be out and about, not closeted at home."
- **Instilling and exploiting a love of nature** - children need opportunities to dig, observe small creatures, wonder at growing plants and create shelters from trees and bushes. Jan White (quoting Rachel Carson) writes that "the lasting pleasures of contact with the natural world are not reserved for scientists but are available to anyone who will place himself under the influence of earth, sea, sky and their amazing life".

The influence of developing theories about learning outdoors

The tradition of outdoor play in early childhood education was a strong one. Over many years it has become buried in what might almost be called neurotic concerns about health and safety; pressures to get young children engaged in formal learning at an earlier and earlier age; and blindness to the benefits of living and learning outdoors. Tovey reminds us that "the onus is on us to play with our inheritance, ensure that it is vibrant, open to new influences, continually reappraised, but not to throw it away, squander it or bury it under a layer of tarmac or rubberized safety surface" (page 52).

Comment

Too often in schools and other early years settings, being outdoors can be limited to playtimes where there are few resources, time available is very restricted and where activities are unplanned and unchallenging.

Adult engagement may be restricted to supervision rather than actually engaging and closely observing what children are doing so that it can be extended and developed. Daniel Walsh (2004 page 105), describing his own child's experience of nursery education in Japan, points out that in Japan supervision of outdoor play is very different. He comments on what initially seemed to him like a lack of care. He describes some tree-climbing:

In one kindergarten the kids liked to climb a tall tree behind one of the buildings. The tree was made for climbing with large, evenly spaced branches. The older kids sometimes climbed quite high, at times making me nervous. The teacher paid little attention and seldom came into this area. I asked the teachers about the tree and how high the kids were climbing. By this time I knew that the teachers cultivated an apparent inattention while being almost clairvoyantly aware of every little thing happening on the playground and off. They had talked about the tree climbing at length in their daily meetings. They decided to ignore it because they didn't want to inhibit the children's explorations and because they were concerned that if they supervised the climbing in any way, the kids would become dependent on them and would, in this dependence, become less careful.

Points for reflection

- Do you agree that learning outdoors is an essential element of children's development?

References

'*Dumbing Down Minds?*' Susan Greenfield (TES 24th November 2006) www.tes.co.uk/article.aspx?storycode=2316539
'Frog Boy and the American Monkey: the body in Japanese early schooling' Daniel Walsh (*In Knowing Bodies, Moving Minds* edited by Liora Bresler) Kluwer Academic Publishers 2004)
Last child in the woods Richard Louv (Algonquin Books 2005)
Learning Outdoors Helen Bilton et al (David Fulton 2005)
Playing and learning outdoors Jan White (Routledge/ Nursery World 2008)
Playing outdoors - spaces and places, risk and challenge Helen Tovey (Open University Press 2007)
Toxic Childhood, Sue Palmer (Orion 2006)

Where to find out more
Learning through Landscapes www.ltl.org.uk
Forest Schools www.foresteducation.org.uk

Moral development

PROFILE

Piaget and Kohlberg are the names most commonly associated with moral development, but a number of other psychologists have researched and written about this vital topic.

LINKS

- *How Children Learn 3*
  Piaget
  Bowlby
  Skinner
  Emotional intelligence
  Gardner

Some key thinking and theories about moral development

Moral education is becoming an increasingly popular topic in the fields of psychology and education. Public anxieties about violence and lawlessness are often focused on young people. In fact morality is a lifelong concern. There are a wealth of theories and in this section some of the most widespread views about the nature of moral development will be explored.

Psychoanalytic theories

Freud claims that the quality of the child's relationship with their parents greatly affects the way the child develops morally. He wrote of the id (the pleasure seeking part of our psyche) and the super-ego (which is our conscience, derived from parents and society). The third aspect he suggested is the ego, helping us to maintain a balance - to find socially (and morally) acceptable ways to satisfy the id.

Robert Emde has written of '*The Dos and Don'ts of Early Moral Development: psychoanalytic traditional and current research*'. He suggests (with some examples) that "guidelines for action (dos) are thought to be learned before prohibitions (don'ts)" and that this occurs in the first and second year of life. He reminds us that psychoanalytic theory is the 'psychology of conflict'. He emphasises the aspects of psychoanalytic theory which he suggests are the roots of morality. They are namely relationships; motives; affect (or emotions); individuality; and psychopathology. This fits with other psychoanalytic writers who also see attachment to others as the basis of morality.

Social Learning Theory

Social Learning theory developed from behaviourism (see *How Children Learn* page 42). Like behaviourism it is assumed that children learn morality by being rewarded or punished. Social learning theory favours the view that children learn morality by imitating adult behaviour. Bandura has undertaken several studies of aggression. The most well-known of these involved a Bobo doll (a figure designed and constructed to be knocked down and then bob up again). In these studies an adult acts aggressively towards a doll and when the adult has left the room, children copy that behaviour. If the adult is seen to be punished for behaving badly, children were less likely to copy that behaviour.

Jean Piaget

In 1932 Piaget published a book entitled *The Moral Judgement of the Child*. Piaget observed children's moral development in two ways. He observed the rules they used and developed in their games. Children up to the age of five simply played for enjoyment, disregarding the rules. Six year olds tended to be inflexible in applying the rules but by the age of ten they realised that rules can be manipulated.

By telling children stories that included a moral dilemma and analysing their responses Piaget suggested that young children were in a stage of moral realism. For them the 'naughtiness' of an action depended on the amount of damage done. A later stage of moral relativism led children to take into account a range of factors - social, personal and cultural. Thus, in a story in which one boy accidentally breaks fifteen cups and another breaks one cup while trying to reach something his mother has placed out of reach, younger children will say that the first is naughtier. Older children will say that the second was behaving less morally because his motives were bad.

Lawrence Kohlberg

Kohlberg is, like Piaget, a constructivist. He built on Piaget's work. By telling stories containing a moral dilemma and asking children what they should do next he concluded that there were three levels of moral development.

In the preconventional level children are initially concerned with avoiding punishment and secondly focused on meeting their own needs. Kohlberg suggested that this included children up to about the age of ten.

After that older children may move to a second level which he called conventional. Initially, their concern is meeting other people's expectations of moral behaviour. The second stage of this level is concerned with doing the right thing for family or groups with which you are closely concerned.

The third level is called postconventional. During this level individuals' behaviour is shaped by the values and opinions of the groups they live and interact with. Moral behaviour is regarded as part of a social contract. The final stage is when universal, moral principles are adhered to. At this stage, a person will obey laws which are consistent with the universal principles but where there is any conflict will stick to principles rather than the social contract.

Nature or nurture?

Robert Coles, the author of the book *The Moral Intelligence of Children* describes children's early years as the 'moral archaeology of childhood'. While acknowledging that babies come in many shapes, sizes and temperaments emphasises that for most babies it is the case that:

> A baby has learned to love, even as it has been loved, to reward with effort those who have exerted effort on its behalf, to accept and please those who have accepted it, have been so pleased by it. This reciprocity of feeling and behaviour, this clear connectedness, as it broadens and enlarges all concerned, is an early expression of a shared respect, a mutuality of regard, a moral mutuality... (1998 page 94)

Cole's book has been praised by Daniel Goleman who wrote *Emotional Intelligence*. Both owe something to the work of Howard Gardner but both emotional and moral intelligence are resisted by Gardner who favours something that he calls existential intelligence. Existential intelligence would involve what he describes as 'ultimate' issues - such as 'the significance of life, the meaning of death' and so on. In a chapter entitled 'Is there a Moral Intelligence?' Gardner (1999) asks the question and concludes that moral behaviour is concerned with the kind of person you are rather than a human intelligence as such.

While Cole clearly thinks of morality as largely nurtured, Gardner's view seems to suggest a balance of nature and nurture. Steven Pinker on the other hand believes, as an evolutionary psychologist, that morality owes much to nature. This doesn't mean that we can excuse immoral behaviour but that our intrinsic morality comes from the structure of the brain. He points to the fact that even toddlers have a sense of sharing and that all cultures have concepts of right and wrong. Pinker compares our innate moral sense to our sense of number—and suggests that both are hardwired into our brain in order to help us deal with complex, abstract ideas. In his view we cannot but think in moral terms.

Putting the theory into practice

Most of the theories described in this section require adults to treat children in moral ways and for the adults themselves to lead moral lives. If you take a psychoanalytical view of morality for example, you will regard secure attachment and helping children to manage feelings in socially acceptable ways as what you must do. Practitioners favouring a social learning viewpoint will place an emphasis on good models of morality, while those favouring learning theory (or behaviourism) will focus on rewarding moral behaviour and punishing unacceptable behaviour.

For constructivists such as Piaget and Kohlberg, accelerating moral development (if that is possible) must be a question of presenting children with moral dilemmas - through story and discussion and in resolving normal daily conflicts. In this way the practitioner creates 'disequilibrium' which children have to resolve through a process of accommodation and assimilation.

Moral development

Cole focuses on kindness to children and supporting secure attachment and emotional well-being. Neither Pinker nor Gardner would argue with that point of view in practice - even though their theories differ from his in some key aspects.

The influence of theories and thinking about moral development

Moral development is much talked about and it would be nice to think that the relevant theories are having influence on practitioners and policy makers. Certainly there is more understanding of the importance of attachment (see for example the Early Years Foundation Stage and the requirement for key persons in all settings). However, there is much room for improvement. Gerhardt (2004) and Palmer (2007), for example, both highlight the way in which current attitudes and practices are placing young children's ability to make strong attachments at risk.

Comment

There are many criticisms of aspects of the theories surrounding the concept of moral development. Both Kohlberg and psychoanalytical theories have been criticised by feminist writers (such as Carol Gilligan). Her work has focused on Kohlberg who suggested that men were more likely to operate at a higher emotional level - thinking in terms of justice rather than care, omitting to take into account emotional aspects of morality.

Both Piaget and Kohlberg have been criticised for being culturally biased in their view of moral development. Although many people have criticized Piaget and Kohlberg about their staged theories of moral development. They are also criticised for reporting development as though it were a one-way, linear process. Do we all act as though we were fully developed in all situations and contexts? Probably not!

It should also be noted that Bandura's Bobo studies have been widely criticised. Critics point out that since the dolls are designed to be knocked down, it is somewhat unfair to label children's behaviour in his study as aggressive. Moreover they were dolls - there can be no certainty that behaviour towards a doll would be replicated with another human being.

Points for reflection
- Do you think moral behaviour can be described as an intelligence as Cole has done - or do you agree with Gardner?

References
The moral intelligence of children Robert Coles (Bloomsbury Publishing 1998)
Intelligence reframed Howard Gardner (Basic Books 1999)
Why Love Matters Sue Gerhardt (Brunner-Routledge 2004)
The psychology of moral development Lawrence Kohlberg (Harper and Row 1984)
Toxic Childhood Sue Palmer (Orion Books 2007)

Where to find out more
http://ehlt.flinders.edu.au/education/DLiT/2000/KESPres/theor.htm%20copy

Postmodernism

Key facts about postmodernism

The fact is, of course, that this term can mean many different things to many different people. To write an exhaustive description would be way beyond the scope of this article. You will often see postmodernism linked to social constructionism, but you will also find it used alongside terms such as post-colonialism, post-structuralism and post-fordism – and this can all be very confusing. Perhaps the simplest way to think about it is to focus on the fact that all these labels are describing theories which attempt to replace previous thinking. In virtually all cases the something that they seek to replace or subvert is the sense of certainty and order, the idea that there is one right way of doing things, that the world is reasonable, rational and predictable.

Glenda MacNaughton describes postmodernism as rejecting the notion of 'the one right way' because the dominant view has brought poverty, war and environmental disaster; and because it has benefited dominant but minority groups in society – both nationally and globally. In addition, she highlights a key feature of postmodernist thinking – namely that it is impossible to describe the world in ways which are true for everybody, at any one time.

Key writing about postmodernism

Foucault was a French philosopher who challenged the idea that there are permanent truths. For him, the discourse or language we use shapes what we regard as valuable or of interest. His views were seized upon by feminists who understood from his work a mechanism by which women throughout history have become marginalized. His writing challenged conventional thinking.

In considering early childhood, the writing of Erica Burman is challenging. This is of course what postmodern writing sets out to do - to deconstruct our assumptions. Burman, like other postmodernists, sets out to deconstruct theories which underpin developmental psychology - such as the work of Piaget and current understandings of young children's social and linguistic development. The work of Gunilla Dahlberg and Peter Moss also takes a postmodern stance and seeks to challenge in particular notions of what constitutes quality, since in postmodernist terms we can only see ideas such as quality from our own cultural perspective.

Postmodern theories

Some key concepts underpinning postmodernism:

- **Othering** describes the way in which dominant groups treat people who they regard as unlike themselves – suggesting superiority rather than simple difference. This may be expressed as being more expert, more able, more creative, more sophisticated and is used to emphasise power relationships. We use 'othering' when we describe certain parents disparagingly; or when we limit expectations of children because of their social class, gender or heritage. A very common criticism of Piaget's work, for example, is that creating an image of 'the child as scientist' has led to the 'othering' of girls – since scientists are stereotypically male.
- **Discourse** in postmodernist thinking is much more than mere conversation. It refers to the way in which we view and construct our world. A discourse both creates and provides a template or framework which is made up of our sense of self in relation to others; our feelings about ourselves and others; the words and images we use to think about and communicate these ideas; and the actions we take as a result. "Who we are, and who we believe we can and should be is created in the particular combination of social templates (or discourses) that we put together for ourselves" (MacNaughton 2003). We all, including children, have many discourses and we constantly make decisions about which one we operate within. Will we be the naughty child or the compliant child; the tomboy, leader or follower?

Postmodernism

- **Seeing what is visible in a different light.** Many postmodernists use the metaphor of lenses or glasses. Moss himself suggests that by using the work in Reggio Emilia as a lens through which to look at our own practice we can 'make the invisible visible'. This simply means that any situation can be interpreted in a number of ways and that we should try out the perspectives (or glasses) used by other disciplines or professionals.
- **Co-construction of knowledge** is a concept which builds on Piaget's notion of constructivism but it goes beyond his initial idea. Co-construction identifies children as 'knowers' who have the ability to co-construct knowledge and culture with adults and peers. Malaguzzi described knowledge as 'a tangle of spaghetti' and consequently in Reggio Emilia learning is regarded as a bundle of 'advances, standstills and retreats that may move in many directions' (Rinaldi cited by Moss), rather than a neat linear progress towards agreed sets of facts. Different people know different truths – which they construct in relation to those around them.

Putting the theory into practice

Peter Moss has tried to challenge or transform thinking about early childhood care and education. Although he has written much about changing the structures of early childhood settings, the real transformation he seeks would come through creating more democratic, listening cultures. This is linked to Gunilla Dahlberg's postmodernist views which highlight both the rights and responsibilities of children. Listening, in relation to work with young children, may be thought of as a way of gauging their interest and seeking genuine understanding. But a postmodern lens requires us to go beyond that simple interpretation and question our views. Who do we listen to? Do we only hear the voices of the dominant (or more powerful) group? Do we only hear those who can speak our language?

These questions are particularly sensitive when considering services for young children. Children want to please adults and can all too easily begin to say what they think we want to hear, making it very difficult to really find out what children are trying to communicate. This is true not simply for babies who have not yet learned to speak but for all the children with whom we work. Adults are more powerful than children and our voices may block out those of the children. This means that we have to be very careful about how we interpret what we hear.

Dahlberg and many other postmodernist thinkers claim that we have an idea of 'the child' in our mind's eye, a prototype which blinds us to individual children. In our interactions we shape such a child

– reinforcing aspects we like and gently eradicating things we don't like. Consider that, for example, "boy or girl?" is the first thing we ask about new-born babies. We do this because we use that information to decide how we relate to them – from birth boys and girls are treated differently.

Peter Moss has written widely about pedagogy. He sees this as more than care and more than education, believing that the care of children shapes their learning and development. Increasingly the successful pedagogue must also be both a reflective practitioner and one who can work effectively with other professionals. Both of these attributes mirror postmodernist ideas. Bolton (2005) describes reflective practice as a 'non-judgemental camera' for which 'no feeling, thought or action is too small or too big for this zoom or wide-angle lens'. Similarly working with other professionals enables practitioners to become aware of a wide range of perspectives.

Although postmodern ideas are challenging there are some key ideas which might be used to guide practice. Think of Malaguzzi's 'tangle of spaghetti' and ask yourself:

- In my work with children am I aware of the ways in which my use of discourse can all too easily lead to bias?
- Do I make use of the range of perspectives offered to me when I work with other professionals?
- Do I monitor and reflect on my own practice to ensure that I really listen to and take account of children's views?

- Do I talk and think about practice with colleagues to ensure that we don't fall into the trap of thinking that there is 'one right way'?

Postmodernist views are complicated and confusing – but they have contributed much to our thinking about equality and the rights of children. If they do no more than encourage you to question what you do, they will have given you a new lens through which to view the world.

- Try to see the world through the eyes of children – valuing their perspectives.
- Active listening demands that we take into account the way in which we listen to and interact with children.
- Work at becoming an even more reflective practitioner, trying to see what you do through the lens or glasses of others.
- Challenge your own thinking, questions your beliefs, interrogate your assumptions, remembering that our views can never be objective.

The influence of post-modern theories

In many ways postmodern theories are too slippery to have a clear influence on practice and practitioners. However, greater understanding of the way in which our use of language shapes our thinking and the way in which certain groups and individuals can be 'othered' or marginalised has impacted on general awareness.

In research there has also been a growing understanding of the way in which our 'norms' can stand in the way of understanding others. Ethnographic research in which the researcher tries to merge with the people or culture being studied draws on postmodern theories.

Comment

Perhaps the aspect of post-modernism that makes it most difficult to engage with is the absence of 'one right way'. This can make it very challenging as we are so used to starting from a set of assumptions. These might be about what high-quality childcare or successful parenting look like, and they almost certainly include ideas about what children ought to be able to do at particular ages. It is far from easy to shed a viewpoint established through training and experience. Views about smiling offer a helpful example: for decades mothers were told (and largely accepted) that their babies were not smiling but had wind, following the invention of video cameras, footage seems to show that babies smile in response to others. Neuroscience has since suggested that this is due to mirror neurons in the brain. Post-modernists on the other hand question whether what we interpret as smiling is that at all!

As this suggests, there is a danger of post-modernists arguing themselves into untenable positions. Many including Dahlberg challenge the basis of developmental psychology. They argue that there can be no 'one right way' to think about development since it will inevitably link with cultural priorities and practices of child-rearing. Morss makes fun of his own criticisms of developmental psychology – saying that if we took his arguments and those of other post-modernists to their logical conclusion we would have to say that babies don't develop! And of course babies do develop – they are not born looking and behaving like adults – for which parents may be eternally grateful.

Although Morss and Dahlberg regularly cite Reggio Emilia as an example of post-modern solutions, those in Reggio Emilia reject any 'isms' (including postmodernism). Rinaldi writes that "'isms' are risky...they simplify and lock you in prison". This, she suggests, takes away the freedom to challenge. Paradoxically, perhaps the strongest criticism of postmodernism is that the constant challenging of widely held ideas could lead to anarchic thinking without theories, without any certainties.

Points for reflection
There is a danger that in rejecting the notion of 'one right way' we become too eclectic - taking only bits and pieces from a number of theories without ever creating a coherent whole. What do you think?

References
Beyond Listening – children's perspectives on early childhood services A., Clark, A.T. Kjorholt, and P. Morss, (eds) (Policy Press 2005)
Beyond Quality in Early Childhood Education G. Dahlberg, P. Moss, and A. Pence (Routledge 2007) (2nd ed)
Shaping early childhood – learners, curriculum and contexts Glenda MacNaughton, . (Open University Press 2003)
The Order of Things: An Archaeology of the Human Sciences Michel Foucault, (Pantheon 1970/ republished Routledge 2002)
The biologising of childhood John Morss (Erlbaum 1990)
Deconstructing Developmental Psychology Erica Burman (Routledge 1994)

Where to find out more
Postmodernism: a very short introduction Christopher Butler (Oxford Paperbacks 2002)

Index

Index